HOW
MUSIC AND
COMPUTERS
WORK

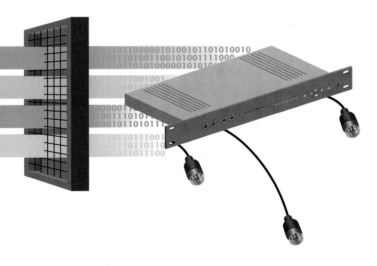

HOW MUSIC AND COMPUTERS WORK

ERIK HOLSINGER

Illustrated by
NEVIN BERGER

Ziff-Davis Press
Emeryville, California

Development Editor	Valerie Haynes Perry
Copy Editor	Kelly Green
Technical Reviewer	Craig Anderton
Project Coordinator	Ami Knox
Proofreader	Carol Burbo
Cover Illustration	Nevin Berger and Regan Honda
Cover Design	Carrie English
Series Book Design	Carrie English
Illustrator	Nevin Berger
Word Processor	Howard Blechman
Layout Artist	M.D. Barrera
Indexer	Valerie Robbins

Ziff-Davis Press books are produced on a Macintosh computer system with the following applications: FrameMaker®, Microsoft® Word, QuarkXPress®, Adobe Illustrator®, Adobe Photoshop®, Adobe Streamline™, MacLink®*Plus*, Aldus® FreeHand™, Collage Plus™.

If you have comments or questions or would like to receive a free catalog, call or write:
Ziff-Davis Press
5903 Christie Avenue
Emeryville, CA 94608
1-800-688-0448

ISBN 1-56276-215-X

Manufactured in the United States of America
✪ This book is printed on paper that contains 50% total recycled fiber of which 20% is de-inked postconsumer fiber.
10 9 8 7 6 5 4 3 2 1

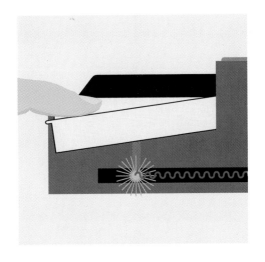

This book is dedicated to my music teachers Dr. Lester Lehr, Dr. Ivan Olson, Dr. Roger Nixon, and Mrs. Mary Torgerson. Their incredible skill, humor, and compassion have forever instilled in me a love of the wonder, beauty, and symmetry of music. No matter how far I delve into computer technology, their teachings will always be a reminder of the real importance of music in my life.

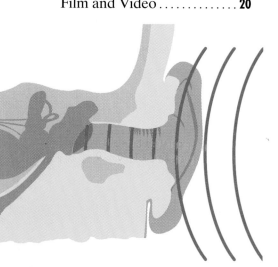

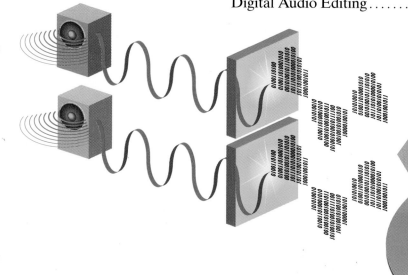

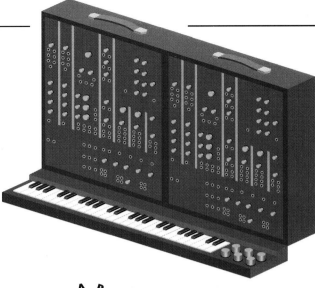

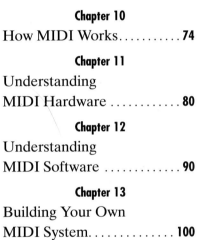

Without a doubt, I owe the greatest thanks to my friend Nevin Berger, the phenomenal artist who did all the illustrations in this book. Nevin's ability to blend incredible illustration skills with a wonderful sense of humor made the grueling production schedule of this book workable. Over the months that we worked together, Nevin never failed to transform my crude sketches and layouts into concise works of art. Even though we jumped from one book project right into another, Nevin never let his enthusiasm, creativity, or steady stream of corny jokes wind down. I salute you, Infographic Specialist del Mundo!

Many people at ZD Press were also invaluable in bringing this book together. Cindy Hudson, the president of ZD Press, and Eric Stone, the acquisitions editor, both deserve a round of applause for making this book and audio CD a reality. I was once again honored to work with Valerie Haynes Perry, the development editor on this book. I'd also like to thank Kelly Green, the copy editor, who worked with Valerie to maintain my style and focus throughout the book. The clarity of the text is a tribute to their candor, patience, and skill.

Ami Knox, my project coordinator, helped keep track of all the last minute corrections and additions. Many thanks go to the gang of rogues that make up the ZD Press art production staff (Steve Delacy, M.D. Barrera, Joe Schneider, Dan Brodnitz, and Charles Cowens). Joe handled all the color prepress work, which is no small job for a book filled with wall-to-wall illustrations. M.D. beautifully integrated my text with Nevin's artwork in page layouts and added a wonderful flair to each image. My thanks and sincere apologies to Howard Blechman, who did the word processing on the book and had to suffer through my arcane handwritten corrections.

I had the great fortune to work with Craig Anderton, a legend in the music industry, who was this book's technical reviewer. Craig's vast experience, honesty, and commitment to clarity provided vital feedback throughout the production of the book. Having read Craig's columns, articles, and books for years, it was an honor to work with him on a book of my own.

Most of this book contains technical information that I gathered from dozens of different sources over the years. While space doesn't permit me to thank all concerned, I'd like to especially give credit to several people who were vital to the completion of this book. Kudos to Marsha Vodovin, public relations expert extraordinaire; OSC, Digidesign, and many music software vendors; and Mark Vail at *Keyboard Magazine*, who patiently helped me with obscure information on a variety of keyboards and used his mighty database to get me much-needed contracts.

Many music hardware and software vendors were invaluable in supplying technical details, software support, loaner equipment, and a lot of encouragement. My thanks to Ralph Goldheim at Roland Corporation; Paul DeBenedictus and Kord Taylor at Opcode; Denny Mayer at Invison Interactive; and Laura Edens at Passport Designs.

I drew from many different works during my research for this book. Some books deserve special recognition for their detailed information on their various audio topics, including the following: *Conceptual Physics* by Paul Hewitt; *Cyberarts*, edited by Linda Jacobson; *The Hearing Loss Handbook* by David M. Vernick, M.D., and Constance Grzelka; *The MIDI Companion* by Jefferey Rona; *MIDI for Musicians* by Craig Anderton; *The Physics of Musical Instruments* by Neville H. Fletcher and Thomas D. Rossing; *Sound Recording Handbook* by John M. Woram; *3D Sound for Virtual Reality and Multimedia* by Dr. Durand R. Begault; and *Vintage Synthesizers* by Mark Vail.

The production of the audio CD came fast and furious after the completion of this book, and I never would have made it had it not been for many folks helping me out. I'd especially like to thank my engineer, director, and friend, Barney Jones at Earwax Productions in San Francisco. His sense of humor, superb aesthetics, and dedication to doing good work made the album a joy to work on. And here's to the rest of the gang at Earwax, which is still the coolest recording studio on earth.

Spending a few months writing a book in Deadline Hell can be very rough on friendships. I'd like to thank my good friends, especially Joan and John Starkovich, Robby and Mabel Robbins, Andres Sender, David and Monica Rudolph, David Hopkins, Polly Smith, Robert Luhn, Bill Meese, and Karen Wickre, for being so patient, caring, and supportive while I went into "Mole" mode during the writing of this book. I would never have been able to complete this book without them.

I'd also like to thank my parents, Eve and Lloyd Holsinger, who put up with miserable playing, late-night practicing, and loud jam sessions for over a decade. Even though my first attempts at playing a clarinet had my dad thinking a demonic goose had moved into the house, both he and my mom supported me through half a dozen different instruments and a plethora of bands. Truly, there is no better example of parental love than to sit through a first-year recital and still remain supportive afterwards.

Finally, I'd like to thank Suzanne Anthony for putting a song in my heart, a light in my eyes, and a smile on my face.

Music is something that everyone can share. It doesn't matter whether you listen to rap, country, classical, or even heavy-metal-rap-rockabilly-classical; there's a tangible *something* about a piece of music that makes you feel good. Whether you play or just listen, music is a reliable haven that you can always turn to when you need to feel better about anything.

Yet many people will cringe when you talk about using music and computers together; suddenly music turns from a nurturing experience to a descent into Technological Hell. Some people react angrily to technology's invasion into music, calling it unnatural or sterile. Others just feel awkward or embarrassed, because they don't understand how to make the two entities work harmoniously. I can understand this viewpoint. Even though I've been composing, performing, and generally fussing with electronic music for many years, sometimes I'm still amazed about how fast music technology changes.

However, you shouldn't let technology get in the way of your enjoyment of music; if anything, it should enhance the experience. I wrote this book to help you realize that in many ways today's music technology makes it easier than ever for you to create music.

How Music and Computers Work is for anyone who wants to understand the many different technologies used in making music with computers. It doesn't matter how much computer experience you have or how familiar you are with electronic music technology. I've tried to keep the text free of jargon, while explaining as many key concepts as possible in an easy, conversational style. Using a variety of graphics, this book will give you a detailed overview of the technologies and uses of electronic music. In addition to explaining basic concepts, I've included a bit of inside information about how professional musicians and producers operate in the field. You'll find out how they use computers and music when recording, playing live, or even creating movie sound effects.

Technology may not be your friend—but it's not necessarily your enemy either. Ultimately, it doesn't matter whether you use computer and music technology or just a pair of spoons; the point is to enjoy yourself. I hope this book will demystify the technology enough so that you can get on with what's really important—making music.

Erik Holsinger
San Francisco, California

MUSIC + COMPUTERS = REAL MUSIC

CONTENTS

OVERVIEW

MOST PEOPLE ASSUME it was only in the last ten years that music became "computerized," yet electronic engineers and scientists have been conducting experiments with computers and music for over forty years. A few beeps, pings, and whirs from a computer the size of a small house were the most you could hope for in the early stages of development, but it was a start. Today the capabilities of computer music systems are astounding, from keyboards with built-in minicomputers that can convincingly duplicate acoustic instruments to computer music setups that can simultaneously play back all the individual parts for an entire symphony.

Some people feel that melding music with computer technology perverts music. A friend of mine once said that *real* music has nothing to do with computers; *real* music has remained untainted by computers and digital electronics. Much to his dismay, I pointed out that it doesn't matter if you listen to rap, bluegrass, classical, heavy metal, jazz, one of the varieties of rock (hard, soft, contemporary, country, modern), punk, or reggae; the fact is that today virtually every type of music involves computers and digital technology. Even if you can't hear it, chances are it's there. You may not hear it because computer and digital technology are there to enhance—and not replace—the quality of your music.

Still, music technology can seem a little overwhelming. The high-tech control rooms of a professional recording studio, with its thousands of lights, dials, and buttons can look more complicated and ominous than the cockpit of a 747 airplane. A computer simply adds to this confusion, making the whole concept of music and computers seem somewhat mysterious. However, once you catch on to a few basic ideas, there is nothing too mysterious about how computers and music work together. In fact, there are only two concepts that you really need to understand: digital audio and MIDI (which stands for Musical Instrument Digital Interface). These are the two main technological breakthroughs at the heart of the music and computer collaboration. Don't worry about understanding these terms now: Just keep them in mind. I'll explain these technologies, how they affect the music that you listen to, and how you can take advantage of them as you go through the book.

You probably are already working with these technologies right now. The first chapter in this section gives you some examples of digital audio and MIDI technology that you probably use around the house. The second chapter shows examples of how professional musicians and recording engineers use digital audio and MIDI when creating records, performing music, or even creating audio effects for television and film. These examples are pretty broad. I've included them to show how intertwined computers and music are in both home and professional systems. These chapters will also introduce you to some key ideas and terms that I'll use throughout the book.

A Crash Course in Digital Audio and MIDI Technology

AS YOU BEGIN to learn about how music and computers work together, the whole subject can seem a little overwhelming. Have no fear because whether you simply own a compact disc player, an answering machine, a home keyboard, or a personal computer, chances are you are already working with digital audio and MIDI technology.

The impact of digital audio is especially widespread. For example, it's probably been a while since you last bought a vinyl record because compact disc (CD) digital audio technology has virtually replaced record albums. CDs have become the listening medium of choice due to their fidelity and longevity, replacing records as surely as audio cassettes killed off eight-track tapes. Even cassettes could eventually become extinct as a recording medium, as Sony and Phillips have released the MiniDisc and DCC (Digital Compact Cassette), respectively. Both of these audio formats can not only play back, but can also record stereo digital audio.

Personal computer systems are also using digital audio and MIDI technology as part of their configurations. Many of these systems also allow you to record CD-quality audio. Most computer systems play back digital audio in games and multimedia CD-ROMs. Even if you just bought your sound board to play games, there is a good chance that you could also use it to play back and record MIDI music. Look closely at the digital audio cards for personal computers and you'll see that they also have a MIDI port for interfacing with MIDI keyboards.

There is one wonderful advantage to today's technology: Music and audio equipment that is available now does much more and costs a lot less than it used to. The push for smaller and cheaper electronics has made high-quality musical and audio equipment more accessible than ever before.

Electronic keyboards are a good example of this trend. When low-cost portable keyboards from Casio, Kawai, Yamaha, and others first came out over ten years ago, they weren't taken seriously because they didn't look as substantial as the bulky wooden consoles of traditional home organs. Yet today some of these under–$1,000 keyboards have more features than the larger, more expensive home organs of yesterday, with even better sounds.

High-end keyboards that you can use at home have features that rival professional keyboards in variety and sound fidelity. For example, Kurzweil's Grand Piano preset sound, an impressive digital recording of a concert grand that was previously only available in their top-of-the-line synthesizer, is now found in the company's line of electronic home keyboards. For less than $1,500, you can now get the sound fidelity that many musicians craved when it was a $10,000 synthesizer.

As you can see, digital audio and MIDI are more common and not as high priced as you might think. As you go through this book, it may take a while to understand the finer points of the technology. Just remember that you are already familiar with the basics of music technology because it is built into many of the things that you have seen or use around the house.

Computers and Music in the Home

Compact Discs   This is the most conspicuous example of digital audio technology. The music that you hear on compact discs uses a technology called *sampling* to convert audio from analog signals into digital form. An analog audio signal uses changes in electrical voltage to represent changes in audio pitch. In sampling, an analog sound, such as a recording of a guitar being strummed, is converted into a series of numerical values, which form the basis of a computer's digital code.

Video Games   Both in the home and in the arcades, those sounds of gleeful destruction and gratuitous violence are actually digital audio sounds that have been sampled and stored in the programming cartridge of the game. While using the same technology as compact discs, the sounds and music for video games are sampled at a much lower resolution, or sampling rate. This allows producers to put many more sounds in a game, as increasing the quality of digital sound also increases the size of the digital audio file.

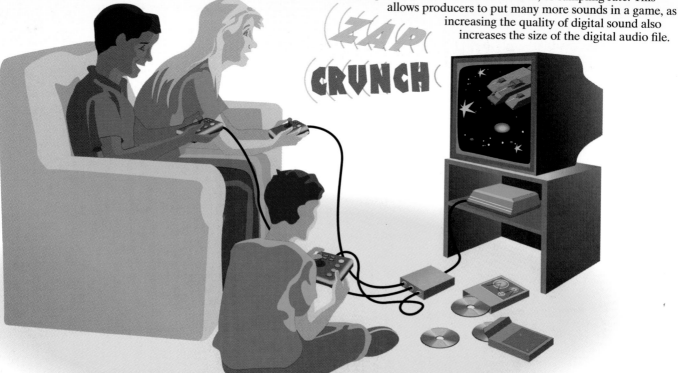

Home Keyboards   There are dozens of home keyboards on the market right now, with built-in rhythm units, auto chords, and other fancy features. While many of these units look like scaled-down versions of home organs, most have an important addition: MIDI in, out, and through ports on the back. You can use these ports to link to other keyboards or to computers. One very popular example of home-based MIDI technology at work is the Miracle Piano System from Software Toolworks, which uses a MIDI keyboard and a personal computer or video game hardware to create a self-paced piano instruction system.

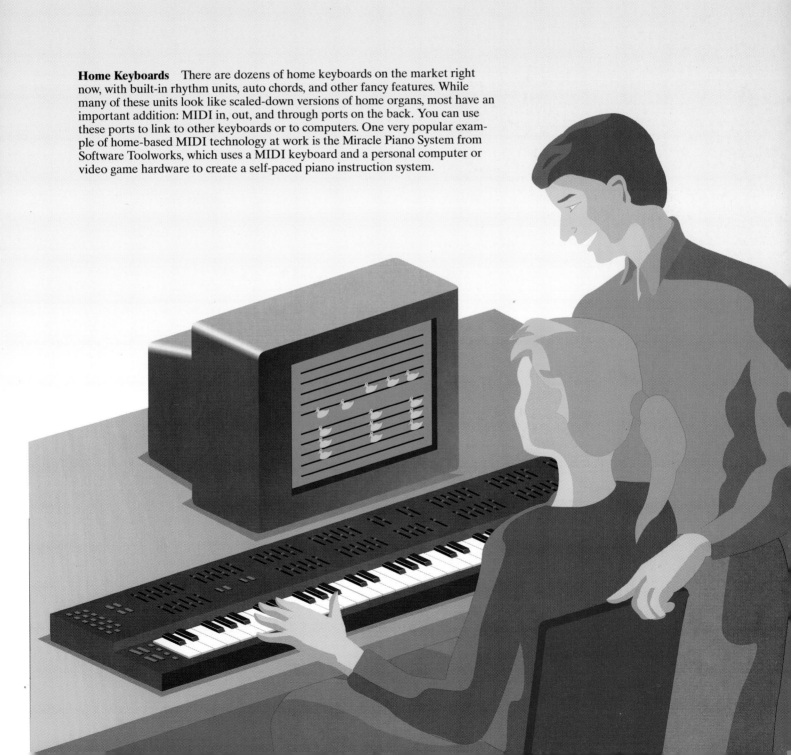

MIDI in Music Composition

ONE OF THE MOST important ways in which MIDI has affected music is in the way it's composed. MIDI is a communications standard created by musical equipment vendors that defines a way for computers, synthesizers, and other electronic equipment to exchange information and control signals. Composers today can create incredibly intricate and professional quality music using various software tools, a personal computer, and MIDI hardware.

At the heart of a MIDI music composition system is a piece of software called a sequencer. This software can either load into a personal computer or be built into a dedicated piece of hardware. A *sequencer* is a kind of word processor for music, where you can record, play back, and edit the performance of different MIDI instruments. A sequencer doesn't actually record sound; it only records and plays back MIDI information, which is the computer data coming from a MIDI instrument. Just think of MIDI data as digital sheet music. MIDI, like sheet music, doesn't actually make music, but contains all the instructions on how to make it: what instrument to use, which notes to play, and how fast and loud to play them.

Composers use sequencers to record MIDI data in the same way that a professional recording studio uses a traditional multitrack tape player: While you are playing a keyboard, the sequencer software records MIDI data coming from the keyboard. Once this MIDI data is in memory, you hit play and send it back out to the keyboard, which plays back the sound just the way you performed it. When you are happy with that part, you can add another that will play back in perfect synchronization with your first track.

MIDI sequencers offer composers several advantages over traditional tape recorders. First is cost: To get a professional system with a good audio mixer and other necessities would bankrupt most musicians, especially when they might not need it all the time. A musician can buy a MIDI music system for a fraction of what it would cost to buy a traditional recording studio. A typical MIDI composing system uses one or more keyboards that have MIDI input and output ports, special MIDI cables, a MIDI interface device to connect the MIDI cable to the computer, and of course, the computer.

Most composers use multi-timbral keyboards or sound modules to play back more than one part from the sequencer. *Multi-timbral* means that the synthesizer or sound module can play back more than one sound at a time, so you can hear several if not all of the different parts of your MIDI sequence simultaneously. The multi-timbral synthesizer does this by assigning each of the parts in the MIDI sequence to a separate sound contained in the synthesizer.

Second, MIDI systems don't use audio tape to record each instrument. This means you can record and play back MIDI music much faster and for much longer. Some systems allow you to record as many parts or as many takes as you'd like; most of the time you are limited only by the amount of computer memory and number of MIDI instruments available.

Finally, the beauty of composing using MIDI is that you are not limited to your own equipment to hear your music. As long as the computer platform and the MIDI software are compatible with your file, you can play back your MIDI file on virtually any MIDI music system. So the song that you composed on your simple MIDI keyboard you can also play back using the $40,000 collection of professional keyboards in a local recording studio. Using MIDI sequencers gives you a cost-effective way to do your composing work at home and just go to the recording studio to finish up your masterpiece.

Music notation software is another important piece of MIDI software for the professional composer. Composers use music notation software to convert their MIDI sequencer files to standard sheet music. With music notation software, composers can print out full scores as well as individual parts for their composition. Once printed out, any traditional instruments or even an orchestra can perform their music. Compared to the old way of handwriting every single part as well as the complete musical score, music notation software can be a godsend.

However, the use of sequencers and music notation software doesn't make writing music any less time consuming or laborious; after all, the word processor didn't make it any easier to write—it only made it a lot easier to clean up typing mistakes and to try out new ideas. The same is true of a MIDI music system; you can quickly try out musical ideas and songs, but that doesn't automatically mean that they are worth listening to.

Still, MIDI and digital audio tools allow you to stretch even further creatively, no matter what level of music education you have. With a little work, nearly anyone can go far beyond the limits of their own musical training or talent to enjoy creating music.

MIDI in Music Composition

Composers use MIDI sequencers to work out musical ideas and performances before they get to the studio. After you have composed a piece of music using a MIDI sequencer, you can take that MIDI sequence on a floppy disk to a professional recording studio and play back your MIDI song using their high-end keyboards and expensive sound equipment. Instead of recording each individual part, you can just play back each part from the MIDI sequencer using the studio's computer and keyboards. Since you've already perfected the MIDI sequence at home, you spend only a fraction of the time and money in the recording studio.

Music score

A composer can convert the MIDI file to regular sheet music using a music notation program. The music notation program changes the notes played, tempo, and other MIDI data to graphic notes, rests, and other musical notation elements. While this process is far from foolproof, it does allow MIDI composers a way to communicate with traditional instrumentalists.

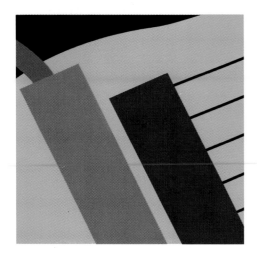

CHAPTER 3

MIDI in Live Performances

AT ONE TIME it was easy to spot the musicians using MIDI technology; they were usually the ones behind stacks of keyboards. Today virtually any instrument you see on stage—guitars, drums, even wind instruments—can be a MIDI instrument. This is because MIDI is very democratic; as long as the data coming in from the MIDI port is a standard MIDI signal, it doesn't matter where it comes from. Consequently, with the right MIDI controller and MIDI instrument, a guitar player can play a hot jazz piano solo or a sax player a sublime bass-guitar line.

Even the audio engineer who mixes sound for a live band can get into the act with MIDI-controlled sound processing equipment. An audio engineer can use a personal computer or some other type of MIDI controller to set up which effects to use and when. This can be a huge relief when engineers have to control multiple sound effects devices; with the right programming, just one push of a button can change the lead singer's reverb setting, add an echo effect to the guitar, and turn the volume down on two of the keyboard player's synthesizers.

Sometimes it is difficult to spot MIDI controllers because musicians sometimes use them in conjunction with regular acoustic instruments. Most drummers use electronic drum controllers in conjunction with a regular acoustic drum set, and the hardware for most guitar synthesizers is mounted on the bridge of the electric guitar.

However, MIDI controllers are not without their problems. For example, some drummers complain that the pads, or rubber striking surfaces, used on many drum controllers are not as responsive as their regular drum set, or that they don't like the sound of digital cymbals when compared to regular cymbals, and so on. Guitarists and wind instrumentalists have similar concerns about guitar and wind controllers; after all, MIDI controllers—especially wind controllers—cannot capture all the nuances of acoustic instruments. Because of this difference, many traditional musicians find that using a MIDI controller is not as comfortable or as flexible as using a traditional guitar, drum, or wind instrument.

Ultimately, it takes a lot of determination and practice to make MIDI controllers work in live performances. Still, many popular musicians have made MIDI work for them in live performances. Keyboard players are still the dominant MIDI users in most bands, but as MIDI controller technology continues to improve, this will change.

MIDI Controllers in Live Performances

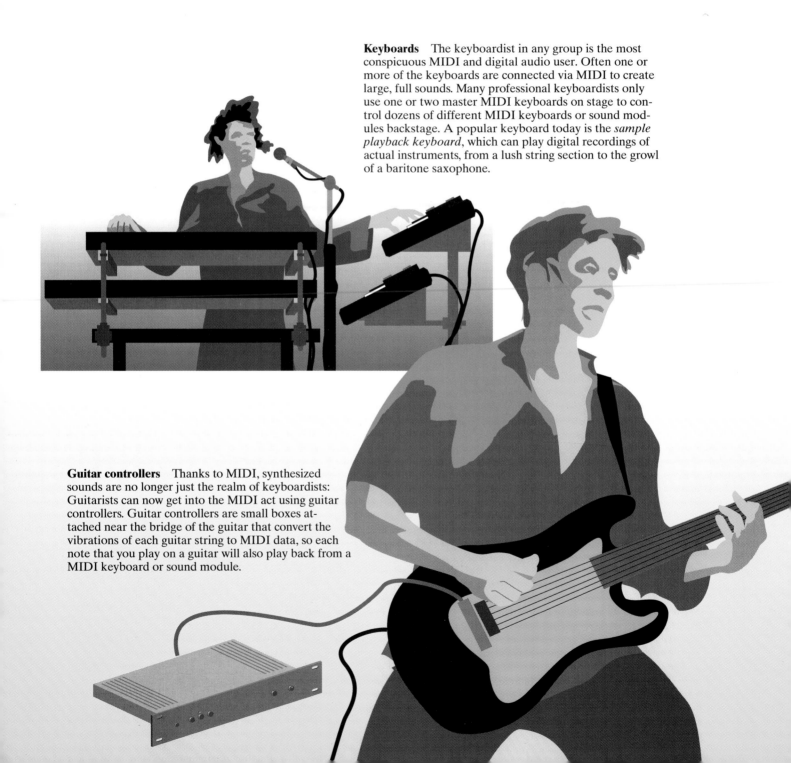

Keyboards   The keyboardist in any group is the most conspicuous MIDI and digital audio user. Often one or more of the keyboards are connected via MIDI to create large, full sounds. Many professional keyboardists only use one or two master MIDI keyboards on stage to control dozens of different MIDI keyboards or sound modules backstage. A popular keyboard today is the *sample playback keyboard*, which can play digital recordings of actual instruments, from a lush string section to the growl of a baritone saxophone.

Guitar controllers   Thanks to MIDI, synthesized sounds are no longer just the realm of keyboardists: Guitarists can now get into the MIDI act using guitar controllers. Guitar controllers are small boxes attached near the bridge of the guitar that convert the vibrations of each guitar string to MIDI data, so each note that you play on a guitar will also play back from a MIDI keyboard or sound module.

Drum controllers   If you notice a live drummer playing drums on what looks like a collection of small rubber pads, chances are they are using a drum controller. Drum controllers allow drummers to control MIDI keyboards and tone modules by converting the impact of a drumstick on a pad to MIDI data. Many drummers also attach MIDI trigger devices to acoustic drums.

Wind controllers   These lightweight devices not only interpret what note to play by what fingering you use, but also determine how loud and how in tune to play a note by how hard you blow into the controller and bite down on the mouthpiece. Wind controllers often use regular fingering that you'd find on a saxophone.

Digital Audio in Film and Video

THERE IS SOMETHING undeniably exquisite and mysterious about the music and sound behind a good movie or television show. Without question, good sound effects and music can make or break a film. Most of the time you'll never notice good film and video sound; but try watching one of your favorite shows with the sound off, and you'll be shocked to learn how much is missing.

Film sound production, for the most part, remains firmly in the realm of nondigital technologies and arcane skills. Take the Foley artist, for example. Anytime you hear someone walking across a floor, opening a door, or making one of a thousand different movements, chances are you are hearing the wondrous work of a Foley artist. A Foley artist realistically re-creates these sounds using special props while watching a synchronized film or video. The skill with which Foley artists precisely match the movement of their sounds with the picture borders on the magical. The sounds of a mad, frantic dash across several hundred feet of desert are easily recaptured by recording a Foley artist running in place in a 2-foot square of gravel.

Various types of sophisticated digital audio and MIDI tools are slowly beginning to find their way into film and video audio production facilities. While many professional sound designers and engineers will agree that there are various benefits to using digital technology, not all of them will give up their older machines to jump onto the digital bandwagon. It really comes down to a matter of economics; if you can't afford to hire a Foley artist to create all of your effects, chances are you can still afford to edit together a few sound effects that were converted to digital computer audio files.

Still, digital audio and MIDI are becoming a big part of film and video production. Perhaps one of the strongest reasons behind the switch to digital audio systems in film and video production is the improvement in theater and home audio systems. Ten years ago you were lucky if the movie theater you went to had stereo; today you can buy a Dolby surround sound system for your home that rivals movie theaters in fidelity. Stereo is an active part of many broadcasts, and the coming of high-definition television (HDTV) is the next evolution in broadcast television. HDTV promises to add four channels of CD-quality digital audio with high-resolution video.

Engineers find that this increase in technology inspires consumers to expect film and video programs that will rely on even more sophisticated audio technology. For now this means a blending of traditional audio tools with digital audio and MIDI technology. However, experts agree that eventually many of the primary tools of audio for film and video will be digital.

Digital Audio in Film and TV

Digital audio and MIDI technology is a big part of film and video production during the *post-production* phase. This phase occurs after all the footage for the film or video has been shot, when the editor assembles all the different takes from the shoot.

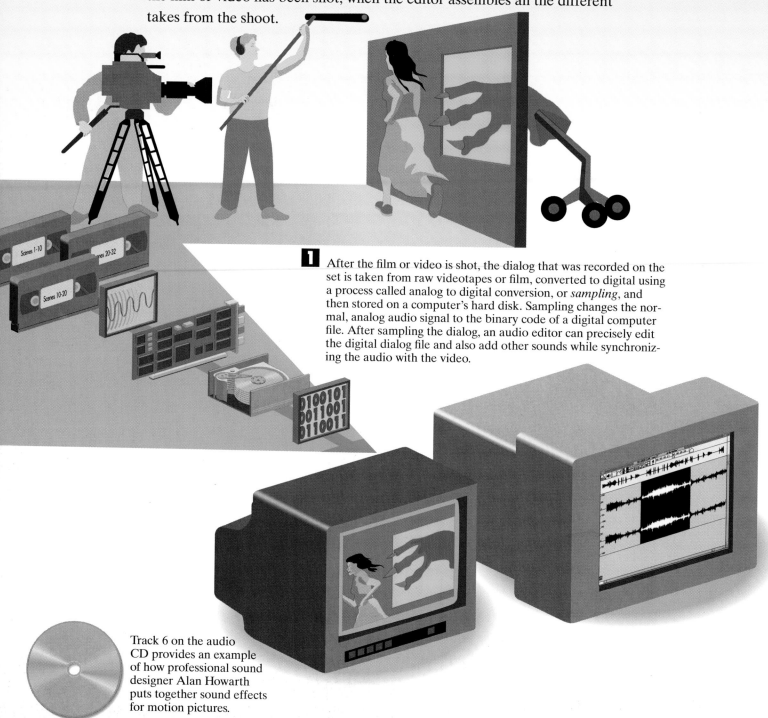

1 After the film or video is shot, the dialog that was recorded on the set is taken from raw videotapes or film, converted to digital using a process called analog to digital conversion, or *sampling*, and then stored on a computer's hard disk. Sampling changes the normal, analog audio signal to the binary code of a digital computer file. After sampling the dialog, an audio editor can precisely edit the digital dialog file and also add other sounds while synchronizing the audio with the video.

Track 6 on the audio CD provides an example of how professional sound designer Alan Howarth puts together sound effects for motion pictures.

2 Once all the different audio elements for the film or video are completed, an audio engineer can digitally combine all the elements using sophisticated digital audio tools and Digital Signal Processing (DSP) technology. DSP technology uses special computer chips that are designed specifically for processing files such as digital audio, digital video, and computer graphics. The engineer can also combine the various digital tracks with MIDI music files that are also synchronized to the video.

UNDERSTANDING
AUDIO TECHNOLOGY

CONTENTS

LIKE MANY ENERGY sources that we work with (electricity, light, gas), sound is a mystery to most of us. There are a few general things that we learn early on: Sound moves slower than light and can reflect off surfaces, and too much is painful. But when it comes to actually figuring out what sound is and how it's created, you might find yourself drawing a blank.

Many people don't think of sound as a powerful energy force. True, when your neighbors play their stereo loud enough to be heard on another continent, it can have a profound effect on your sleep; yet it's not as serious as a lighting storm or a gale-force wind. Still, the effect of sound on you and your environment can be both subtle and devastating.

For example, scientists, researchers, and horror movie directors found that certain types of tones create feelings of anxiety or fear. Just think of all the times you have heard a high, sustained note during a tense moment in an action or horror film. The high note is a similar but more subtle version of scratching your fingernails on a blackboard; instead of causing an immediate reaction, the sustained note causes a feeling of anxiousness.

For a more obvious example of sound power, have you ever seen a movie where someone sings a high note and shatters a glass? This happens when the high note matches the resonant frequency or natural vibration within the glass, causing it to vibrate so strongly that it explodes. This process, called *resonance*, can have a dramatic effect on even larger objects. For example, in his book *Conceptual Physics*, Paul Hewitt relates how in 1831 a cavalry troop marching across a footbridge near Manchester, England caused the bridge to collapse due to resonance. Apparently, the rhythmic sound of the marching troops matched the bridge's resonant frequency, causing a vibration that tore the bridge apart. Now troops have to make sure that they don't march in step when they cross this kind of bridge.

There are a lot of misconceptions about how sound works. For example, some people believe that yelling loudly in a very shrill voice during a baseball game will get their sound to the offending player or umpire faster. However, every sound travels at the same speed. Sound can move very fast (close to 1,200 kilometers per hour), but its quality can be affected by wind conditions, temperature, and humidity.

A little understanding of how sound works can go a long way. How many times have you seen an ad for a piece of stereo equipment that bragged about how it had over 90 dB of dynamic range, 20 Hz to 20 kHz frequency response, and so on—and had no idea what the ad was talking about? People in stereo stores often will confuse you with technical specifications that may or may not make any difference to you. Just because a stereo system gives you a super high-frequency response doesn't mean that you are physically capable of hearing it.

The next few chapters discuss some of the basics of sound, especially the areas that affect digital audio. Chapter 5 deals with the basic elements of sound, and Chapter 6 explores the limits of our hearing. This will give you some audio background that will help you understand some of the concepts I talk about in Part 3.

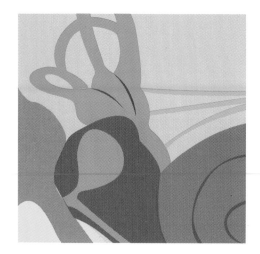

How Sound Works

SOUND IS A form of energy, in some ways just like light or electricity. Sounds are simply waves created by vibrations in different objects. When we talk, the vocal cords in our throats vibrate. In music, you can create these vibrations in a thousand different ways, by plucking a guitar string, blowing through a trumpet mouthpiece, dragging a bow across a violin string, and so on.

There are two main components to sound; frequency and loudness (also called force). The *frequency* and *pitch* of a sound are directly related to how fast the object vibrates. Frequency is measured in *hertz* (Hz), which determines the number of vibrations that occur in 1 second. When you push down on the A key above middle C on a piano, a hammer inside the piano strikes several strings. Once struck, each of these strings vibrates 440 times each second; this means the frequency of the A note you've just struck is 440 Hz. Lower-frequency sounds—such as tubas and bass guitars—have fewer vibrations per second, so they sound lower.

It is important to point out that frequency and pitch are not exactly the same thing. While frequency is an exact physical parameter, pitch is more strictly a musical parameter: In some cases the same pitch can be different frequencies.

The loudness, or force, of sound is measured in decibels (dB). (*Deci* means *ten* and *bel* is a tribute to Alexander Graham Bell, the inventor of the telephone.) The decibel scale is logarithmic, or exponential, which means that every 20 decibels increases the amplitude, or volume, of a sound 10 times: so the sound of striking a 60 dB snare drum is 10 times louder than a 40 dB sound, while an 80 dB cymbal crash is 100 times louder than a 40 dB sound.

Nearly all sounds produce fundamental tones. A *fundamental tone* vibrates exactly at a specific frequency or note. If you've ever struck a tuning fork and held it up to your ear, you've heard this clear, pure tone.

The reason that every instrument doesn't sound alike is because of additional elements, or tones, that are added to the sound. These additional tones are called the harmonic series and they determine the complexity of a sound. For example, a guitar sounds different from a banjo or a clarinet because of the harmonic series. The fundamental frequency in a musical sound is where the most sound energy is concentrated; the rest of the energy is spread out in various amounts to the other harmonics.

It is easier to understand how harmonics and fundamentals interact if you think of ripples on a pond. If you toss one pebble into the middle of the pond, the ripples that result move out perfectly from the middle in a nice circle. This is how a pure fundamental behaves. However, if you throw in one big stone and several smaller ones simultaneously, the ripples aren't even. The same happens when you mix a fundamental tone with one or more harmonic tones: Instead of a pure tone, the combination of fundamentals and harmonic series produces variations in the sound. Several factors determine the resulting number of harmonic tones in this instance. These factors include the way in which you create the note as well as the resonant qualities of your instrument.

Many computer programs that work with digital audio can graphically show you the complexity of a sound by displaying a waveform. A *waveform* draws a line that moves up or down according to the frequency and the loudness of the sound as it plays back. When displayed, a waveform can give you a lot of information about the complexity and nature of a sound.

The Elements of Sound

Here's a quick look at what sound is made of and how we hear it. This will give you a good understanding of terms and concepts used in the next section on digital audio.

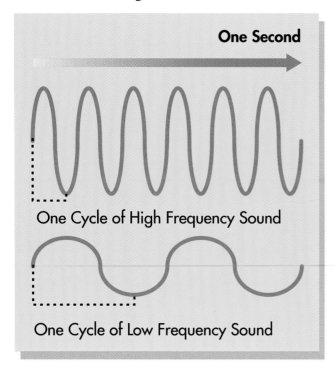

One Second

One Cycle of High Frequency Sound

One Cycle of Low Frequency Sound

Sound is a form of energy that moves in waves created by an object vibrating. When the object vibrates quickly, it puts out a high-pitched sound; when it vibrates slowly, it produces a low-pitched sound. The pitch, or *frequency,* of the sound is measured in cycles per second, or hertz. The graphic to the left shows one complete cycle, or "wave."

When you use an instrument to create a sound, the fundamental tone of a sound combines with different harmonics, or additional tones. Without this blending, all instruments and voices you hear would sound similar. This interaction can be recorded in a complex waveform. A waveform draws a line that moves up and down according to the frequency and loudness of a signal as it is played back. Waveforms are built into many applications for digital audio.

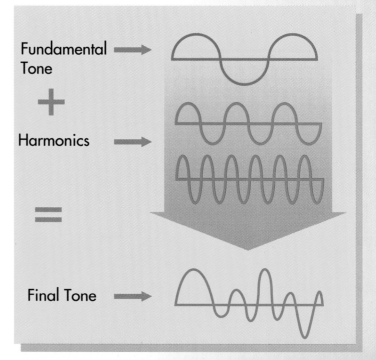

Fundamental Tone

+

Harmonics

=

Final Tone

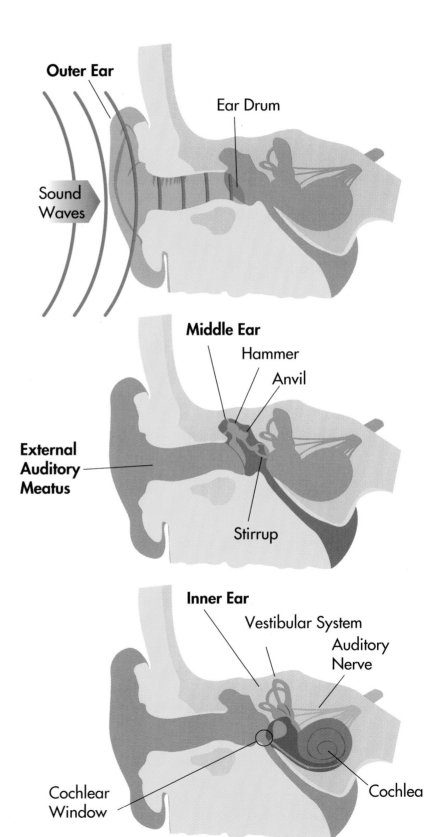

The Outer Ear   When you play a note, the vibrations of that sound travel through the air and are funneled into the ear canal, which is known as the external auditory meatus. The ear drum vibrates as the sound energy hits it. These physical reactions change the vibrations in the air into mechanical energy.

The Middle Ear   Just past the eardrum you'll find three small bones, called the hammer (or malleus), anvil (or incus), and stirrup (or stapes). Once the eardrum starts vibrating, these bones redirect the energy of those vibrations and intensify them. The stirrup bone collects and focuses these vibrations into the opening of the inner ear, which is called the oval, or cochlear, window.

The Inner Ear   The inner ear is filled with fluid. When the stirrup causes the cochlear window to vibrate, this creates waves in the fluid. Thousands of tiny hair cells within the cochlea become electrically charged when these fluid waves move past them. These interactions send a message to the brain via the auditory nerve. When the message is received, a sound is registered. We keep our balance thanks to the vestibular system inside the inner ear, which uses three fluid-filled canals to update the brain on our position.

Understanding Stereo and Three-Dimensional Audio

1 Stereo is the term assigned to sounds that rely on two discrete speakers for balance and playback. When you put on a pair of stereo headphones, sound permeates your environment. In fact, whatever you listen to may have the effect of transforming your environment. The science of psycho-acoustics is concerned with this phenomenon. Psycho-acoustics is not music for the insane, but actually a science that studies how people perceive sound. Research in this field has identified four factors that determnine how we locate sound.

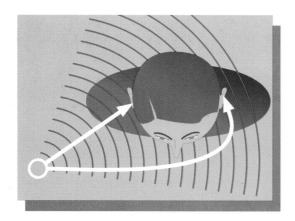

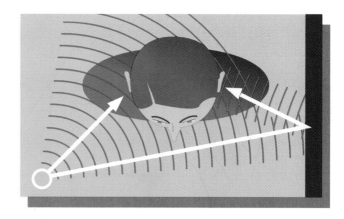

2 The first two factors are interaural time and intensity differences. The *interaural time difference* is the difference in time that it takes each ear to hear the same sound. The *interaural intensity difference* refers to the amplitude difference at each ear.

3 The shape of your outer ear also affects sound localization by causing sound wave reflections; each ear shape affects sound differently.

4 Because ears are located on opposite sides of the head, one ear is initially blocked from a sound. This effect is called *head shadowing*. In other words, one ear hears a sound primarily through reflections of the original sound. The combination of these factors helps you determine the location of a sound.

5 3D audio is a new branch of audio science. It attempts to re-create an audio environment that simulates not just right and left depth, but can also place sounds above, below, and moving at any distance from the listener. Using sophisticated audio processing technology, scientists are working on 3D audio technology for virtual reality systems and home entertainment. At NASA Ames Research Center, Dr. Durand R. Begault is developing a traffic avoidance system that uses 3D sound for airline pilots. Instead of just seeing a visual warning that you are about to crash your 747 into another plane, the 3D audio system would give you an audio warning that placed the sound in the approaching plane's location. This would give the pilot and copilot auditory pointers as to where collisions might occur.

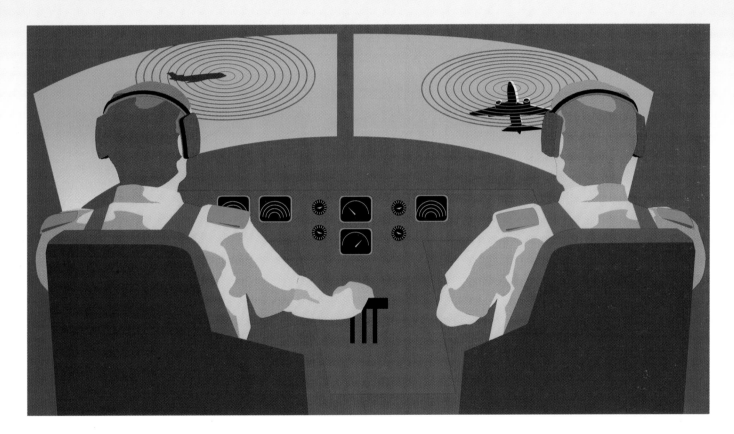

To give you an example of what 3D audio is like, Dr. Durand Begault and I have put together a short demonstration of 3D audio at work. Just play track 9 on the audio compact disc. For best results, you should listen to this demo with headphones.

The Range of Human Hearing

I N SPITE OF the improvements of various audio technologies, there are limitations in our hearing that must always be considered.

Humans can hear within the range of 20 hertz to 20,000 hertz or 20 kHz. We are most sensitive to sounds around the 1 kHz to 4 kHz frequency range, which corresponds to the range of typical conversation. Sounds that occur above 20 kHz are called ultrasound.

Many animals can hear ultrasounds; dogs, for example, can hear sounds as high as 35 kHz. That's why when you blow on a dog whistle, you can't hear anything; the whistle is vibrating at a frequency too high for you to perceive.

Today ultrasound is used extensively in the medical field, where doctors use it to detect heart abnormalities, blood clots, and tumors. Doctors also use ultrasound to treat stiffness in joints and even safely check on an unborn fetus to make sure that everything is okay.

Sounds that occur below 20 hertz are called infrasound. Infrasounds are naturally produced in earthquakes.

Something that you'll often see described in the technical specifications of stereo equipment is a dynamic range. Some companies boast products that have a dynamic range of over 90 dB. Because dB, or decibel, level is measured logarithmically, a 90 dB dynamic range means the loudest sound will be about 30,000 times louder than the softest sound. This is important when the music you play ranges from very soft to very loud; classical music—especially symphonic works—is a good example of music that requires a wide dynamic range. The reason you hear about dynamic range more than ever is that unlike most cassette players and some record players, CD players can achieve a wide dynamic range.

Loudness is also an area in hearing where we just aren't well equipped. While the hammer and the stirrup bones inside the middle ear can help mute loud sounds, they can't protect you against sudden noises, such as a firecracker going off very close to you. Constant exposure to loud decibel levels can cause permanent hearing loss, which is why you'll see people working out on the runways of airports wearing special headphones: Without this protection, the noise of the aircraft would quickly deafen them.

The Range of Human Hearing

Human hearing is good, but many animals can hear much better. Hearing is at its peak during childhood, with the potential to hear as low as 20 Hz and as high as 20 kHz; most adults can only hear sounds up to around 17 kHz or so, and often much less.

Sonar was one of the first practical human applications of ultrasound. It was put on board ships to find objects underwater, such as submarines. Sonar works by sending out a high-frequency sound and measuring the echoes that come back. This process, called *echolocation*, is similar to what bats and dolphins use to catch food and avoid crashing into objects while they are flying or swimming.

Ultra Sound

35 Khz

25 Khz

20 Khz

11 Khz

4 Khz
1Khz
500HZ

200HZ

100HZ

50HZ
20HZ
10HZ

Infra Sound

There are many potential sources of high-decibel sounds. While you can take these sounds in small doses, it's best to avoid long exposure to any sounds over 90 dB. Keep in mind that an intense short sound can cause you harm. For example, a direct blast from a jackhammer can be just as damaging as an evening spent in a loud rock concert.

140 Decibel Level

120

Threshold of Pain

90 100—

115

Loud Rock Concert

Normal Conversation

60

Whisper

30

0

Lowest Audible Sound Heard by the Human Ear

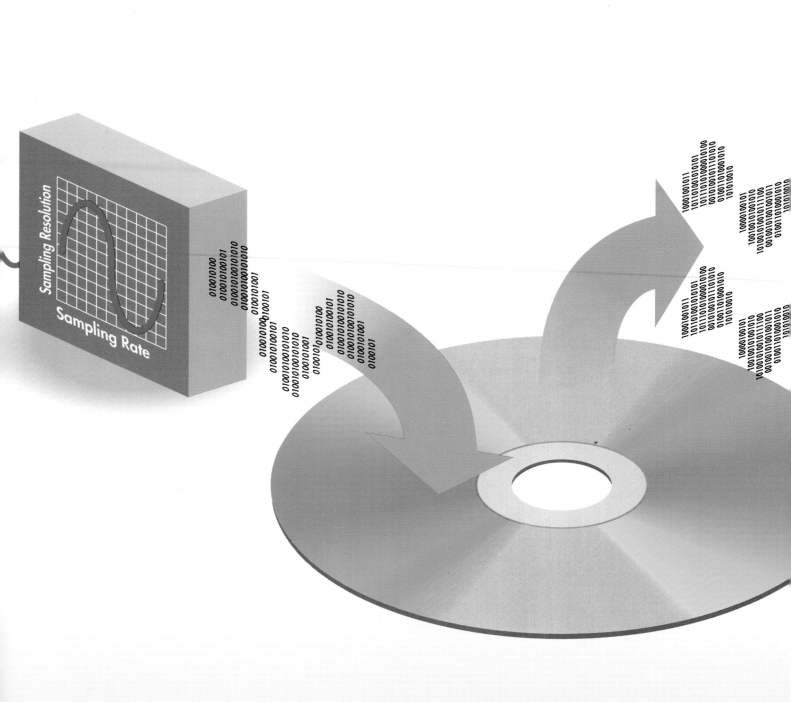

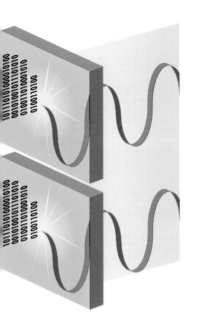

3

UNDERSTANDING DIGITAL AUDIO

CONTENTS

DIGITAL RECORDING TECHNOLOGY has been around for over a decade. Sampler keyboards, or samplers, were one of the first musical uses for digital audio technology. Samplers could take a recording of any instrument or sound—from a violin to a dog barking—and play it back from a musical keyboard. Playing the note higher or lower raises or lowers the pitch of the sound, so musicians can play back melodies with the sound.

Naturally, this technology didn't come cheaply. It has only come into the price range of the average person within the last few years. When the first dedicated keyboard sampler—the Fairlight CMI (computer music instrument) from Fairlight Instruments—came out in 1979, it cost over $25,000. Used by musicians during the early 1980s, this heavy-duty instrument could play eight notes at a time and was controlled by a special monitor screen with a light pen; to change a sound parameter or select a new sound you would literally touch the screen using the pen. If you were a world-class musician like Peter Gabriel, Kate Bush, or Michael Jackson, then the Fairlight's expense was justifiable; but at that time, the Fairlight was something most musicians only dreamed about.

Yet like most technology, it was only a matter of time before the cost came way down. It was just five years later when the Ensoniq Mirage, the first mass-market sampler, took the music industry by storm with a list price of only $1,695. The Mirage offered many of the same capabilities and sound quality as the original Fairlight at a fraction of the cost. Needless to say, the Mirages sold as fast as Ensoniq could build them. Today you'll find sampler keyboards and systems used in everything from the blues-based rock and roll of ZZ Top to some of the hottest rap music around today.

Digital audio is not only for music. You might think that compact discs are the main example of digital audio, but this technology is much more widespread. In fact, digital audio has become as ubiquitous with the general public as the telephone.

Chances are you hear an example of digital audio at least once a day. For instance, if you played a video game, or left a message on voicemail or an answering machine, you probably heard an example of digital audio. The various grunts, splats, and shouts in a video games are often digital recordings added to the program. Some game systems, such as the Real 3DO Interactive Multiplayer from Panasonic, also include a digital music sound track. Many answering machines and most voicemail systems use digital audio systems to answer your call and record your message. When you leave a message, you are actually leaving a digital audio file on a computer hard disk attached to the voicemail system.

Those stiff recordings that come on after the directory assistance operator finds your number are another good example of digital audio; a voice gives you the number, but it is obvious that the numbers are pieced together using separate digital recordings of numbers. You can even find greeting cards that use digital audio technology to record a message on a small chip inside the greeting card.

Chapter 7 discusses how audio is digitized. *Audio digitizing* involves converting the electrical energy of the standard analog audio signal to a digital computer code made up of 0s and 1s. The two key factors are digitizing the analog audio signal and later converting the digital signal back into an analog audio signal during playback. This chapter will help you understand these concepts so you'll have a good handle on how digital audio is created and played back.

Chapter 8 covers digital audio in personal computers, a new market for digital audio technology that has exploded over the last few years. Here we'll look at how the audio cards that you can buy for your PC work, and we'll also look at DSP (digital signal processing) in PCs.

Finally, Chapter 9 explores the hardware and software process of editing digital audio. This technology is often found in television and motion picture production, as well as in the music industry.

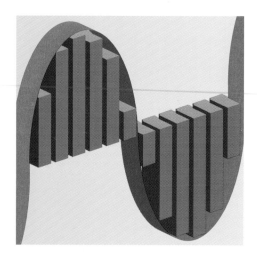

CHAPTER
7

Digital Audio Recording

DIGITAL AUDIO MAY sound very high tech and arcane, but it's really very simple when you break it down. There are two main differences between regular analog audio and digital audio: how the sound is recorded and how it is played back. Analog sound is recorded by transferring electrical energy onto a magnetic medium, such as cassettes and videotape, or a vinyl medium, such as a record album. On a cassette, the electromagnet in the record head of the cassette fluctuates according to how much current is passing through it. As the magnetic tape moves past the record head, these fluctuations are imprinted on the tape. When the sound is played back, the playback head reads the magnetic imprint on the tape and produces an electrical signal similar to the original sound.

Digital sound is recorded by means of a process called sampling. *Sampling* converts the electrical energy from a regular analog audio signal to the binary code of 1s and 0s, also called *bits*, that make up a digital audio file. The main hardware involved in sampling is an analog to digital converter (also called an A-to-D converter), which samples the audio signal.

An audio sample is similar to a frame of motion picture film. An entire sample is made up of individual samples that each describe part of the sound. A single frame of film or a single audio sample won't tell you much about what motion is in the film or what the audio sounds like. However, once the many samples are played back very quickly in sequence, you get the illusion of a whole sound. Likewise, when you see frames assembled as a film, you perceive moving images.

The sample creates a graph of the audio waveform, which was caused by the vibration and harmonics of the sound. This mathematical description of the sound is saved onto a computer storage device, such as a hard disk. When you want to play back the sound, the computer data is sent through a digital to analog (D-to-A) converter, which changes the digital code back into an analog signal.

Two main factors affect the quality of a digital recording: the sample rate and the sample resolution. The *sample rate* is how often the waveform is measured every second, and the *sample resolution* determines the precision of those measurements. Think of it this way: If we still think of a sample in film terms, the sample rate would be the frame rate of the film and sample resolution would be the focus. Together or separately, these two factors play a big part in determining the quality of the digital audio.

Many sampling units have sample rates as high as 48 kHz, and even audio CDs are sampled at a resolution of 44.1 kHz. These ranges are far higher than humans could possibly hear, so why bother? A mathematical principal called the Nyquist Limit is the justification. *The Nyquist Limit* is a scientific principal that definitively proved that in order for a sample to precisely re-create a sound, the sample rate must be twice as high as the highest frequency in the sound. Since we can't hear above 20 kHz, it is a safe bet that a sound sampled over 44.1 kHz will accurately reproduce the sound.

Yet a digital sound doesn't have to have a high sampling rate to be good or usable. For example, when a voicemail system records your voice, it doesn't sample your voice at 44.1 kHz; in fact, it's likely to use something much lower, probably 22 kHz. Since a speaking voice is usually no higher than about 10 kHz, a sampling rate of 22 kHz can accurately reproduce your voice when playing back the message. The reason people reduce sampling rates is simply to save on memory; the lower the sampling rate, the less computer hard-disk storage the sound takes up. Sample rate reduction is a good way to stretch the capacity of your system.

How Audio Is Digitized

Digitizing is another way of describing sampling. It connects analog data (such as audio, video, or even still images such as photographs) to digital computer code. For example, a microphone can convert the acoustic energy of someone talking into electrical energy. This energy takes the form of a low-voltage signal that is then routed to a digital recorder. The signal is put through the analog to digital (A-to-D) converter, which measures the incoming audio many times every second according to the sampling rate of the recorder.

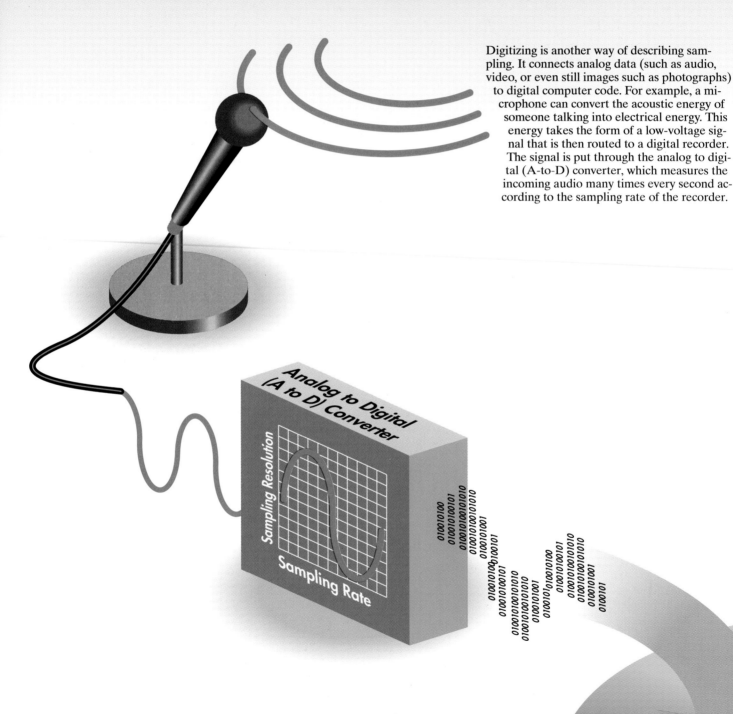

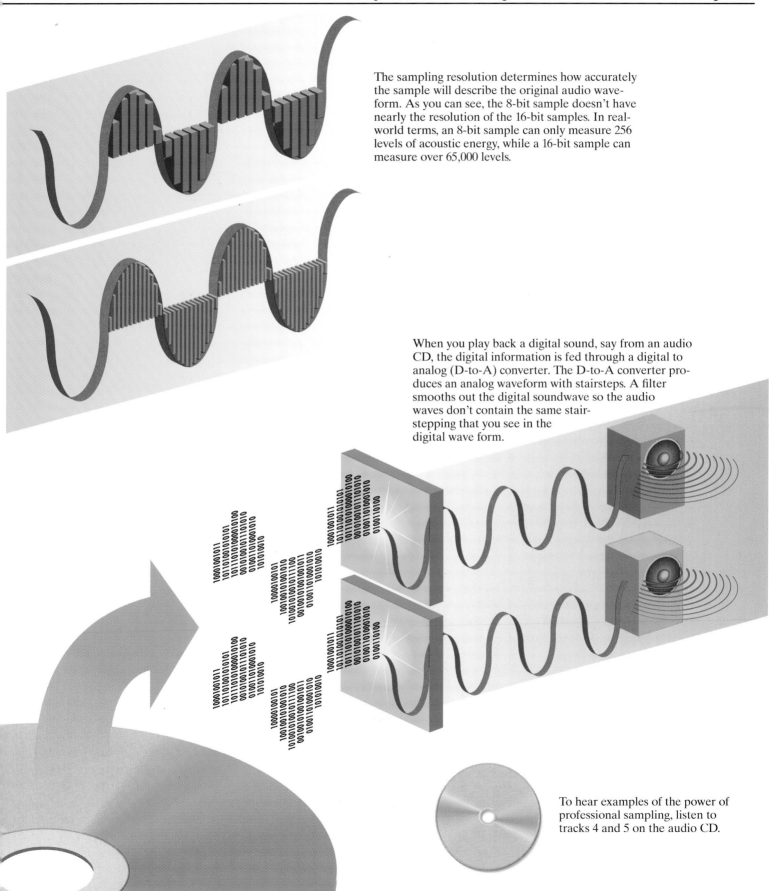

The sampling resolution determines how accurately the sample will describe the original audio waveform. As you can see, the 8-bit sample doesn't have nearly the resolution of the 16-bit samples. In real-world terms, an 8-bit sample can only measure 256 levels of acoustic energy, while a 16-bit sample can measure over 65,000 levels.

When you play back a digital sound, say from an audio CD, the digital information is fed through a digital to analog (D-to-A) converter. The D-to-A converter produces an analog waveform with stairsteps. A filter smooths out the digital soundwave so the audio waves don't contain the same stair-stepping that you see in the digital wave form.

To hear examples of the power of professional sampling, listen to tracks 4 and 5 on the audio CD.

Analog Sound versus Digital Audio

Analog and digital audio both offer advantages and disadvantages according to how you intend to use them. Analog media record audio as a magnetic impression of electrical signals on magnetic media, while digital media record audio as binary computer code on a variety of media. Here's a comparison of some of the different types of analog and digital media available.

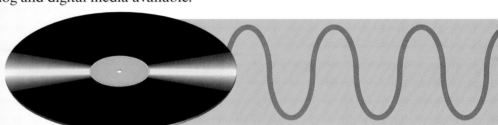

Records   Once the standard for playing back music, the vinyl record is easily damaged by heat, scratches, and constant use. Vinyl records also have a limited frequency response, and are subject to certain playback distortions of sound.

Cassettes   Still the handiest and least expensive way to play back recorded music in your car, most cassettes have a limited frequency response and are often devoured by hungry tape players.

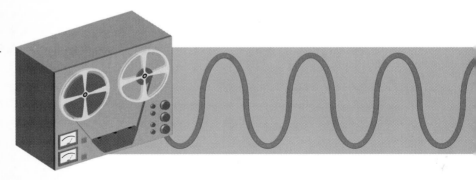

Reel-to-Reel Tape   Still used as the main recording decks in professional recording studios, reel-to-reel tape decks offer superb audio fidelity. The main drawback (besides price) of a good reel-to-reel machine is that it is difficult to find specific sections on the tape. However, some decks are equipped with an autolocator feature.

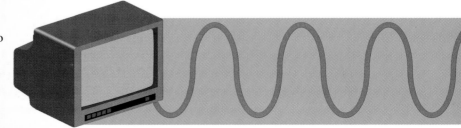

Television   Today you can hear stereo on cable and some television stations that broadcast stereo programs. However, the fidelity is still poor because these sound improvements have to be added into the original TV specification, which hasn't changed since 1951.

10011101000101010010010101010˙
00111000110101010100111110
010110001100110010101011010

Compact Discs The successor to records, audio CDs offer better fidelity, lower noise, and more music than vinyl records (up to 74 minutes per compact disc). However, CDs are also somewhat fragile; scratching the bottom surface or leaving a CD in the sun will make it unplayable.

1001110100010101001001010101010˙
0011100011010101010100111101001101˙
010110001100110010101011010110101˙

Mini-Disc (MD) and Digital Compact Cassette (DCC) These two new formats from Sony and Philips, respectively, are vying for the cassette/personal recorder market. The Mini-disc (MD) uses a magneto-optical disc to record audio; the DCC uses special magnetic tape inside cases that resemble standard cassettes. Both systems have the advantages of being digital (long life, good fidelity, and so on), but MD and DCC hardware costs more than cassettes. However, both systems compress their audio. This means their fidelity is not as good as CDs or DAT.

1001110100010101001001010101010010˙
0011100011010101010100111101001101˙
010110001100110010101011010110101˙

Digital Audio Tape (DAT) You'll find DAT in use at recording studios and production houses; there are also a variety of low-cost consumer units available. Unlike MD and DCC technology, DAT recordings don't compress the audio at all, so the sound fidelity is CD-quality. You can also record markers onto DATs so it is easy to locate specific sections of the tape later on. The main down side of DATs is that they are still susceptible to damage by magnetic fields, dust, aging, accidents, and misuse.

10011101000101010010010101010010˙
0011100011010101010100111101001101˙
010110001100110010101011010110101˙

High Definition Television (HDTV) The latest evolution in television technology, the digital signal of HDTV promises to add four channels of CD-quality sound. Broadcasters can use these four channels for surround-sound programs, or as additional language channels. Unfortunately, it will be some time before HDTV replaces regular television, due to the cost of hardware and the lack of a definitive standard.

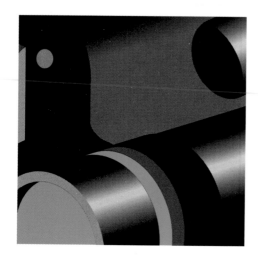

How Personal Computers Use Digital Audio

DIGITAL AUDIO IN computers has taken some time to get to the public. Early personal computers could barely get out a beep tone from a small internal speaker. Today, some personal computers have replaced beep tones with the first notes of a symphony or the screech of a car crash by incorporating digital audio into their system. Since a digital audio file is really just computer data, it should be easy for a computer to play back digital audio, right? Well, the answer is yes...and no.

True, you should be able to read digital audio files from within a computer. Unfortunately, like many aspects of computers there is a problem with the format of the sound file. Each computer system uses a sound file format that works specifically with its own platform. The Mac uses the SND (Sound) file format, and Windows uses the .WAV file format; both are 8-bit sample formats that have an upper sampling rate limit of about 22 kHz, yet they are completely separate, incompatible formats. You must use a separate software utility program to convert a file from one format to another, in order to play back the file.

Not every personal computer can play back all types of digital sound files. For example, an *audio interchange file format* (AIFF) sound file won't play back on most systems; you'll need an external audio board to do this. These files are more difficult to process than the SND or .WAV files, because AIFF sounds can contain higher-resolution samples; unlike SND or .WAV files, you can save AIFF files with sample rates of 44.1 kHz or higher. In sound quality, this is a huge difference; music sampled at 44.1 kHz sounds incredibly good, while the same music sampled at 22 kHz sounds like it's being played over a telephone.

The main ingredient missing from most computers that a third-party audio card provides is a DSP (digital signal processing) chip. The DSP chip is a special processor that can do blindingly fast calculations on certain types of data, such as digital audio, digital video, and graphics. The DSP chip takes the pressure off the computer's brain (also called the CPU, or central processing unit), so that the digital audio file plays back smoothly. Some computers, such as the AV series of

Macintosh computers and the Silicon Graphics Indy, have a DSP chip built-in; using this DSP chip, you can play back high-resolution AIFF files without any third-party card board.

The good news about audio cards is that you can buy a high-quality audio board for a fraction of what it once cost. Whereas the first computers that could process digital audio were expensive workstations, today for well under $2,000 you can buy a digital audio board for your Mac or PC that can record and play back CD-quality sound. As the cost of digital technology decreases and more computers come with built-in DSP chips, it is likely that CD quality will replace the lower-resolution digital audio common in today's line of personal computers.

How Computers Play Digital Audio

Each computer platform varies in how it plays back digital audio files from within its system. This example is common with most Macintoshes and some PCs; however, many PC-based computers require the use of an audio sound card to play back any kind of digital audio file.

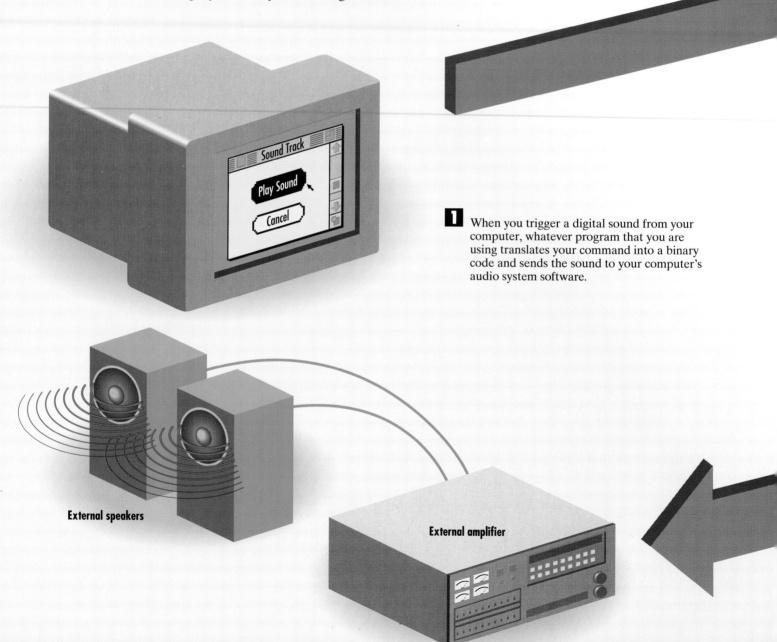

Sound Track

Play Sound

Cancel

1 When you trigger a digital sound from your computer, whatever program that you are using translates your command into a binary code and sends the sound to your computer's audio system software.

External speakers

External amplifier

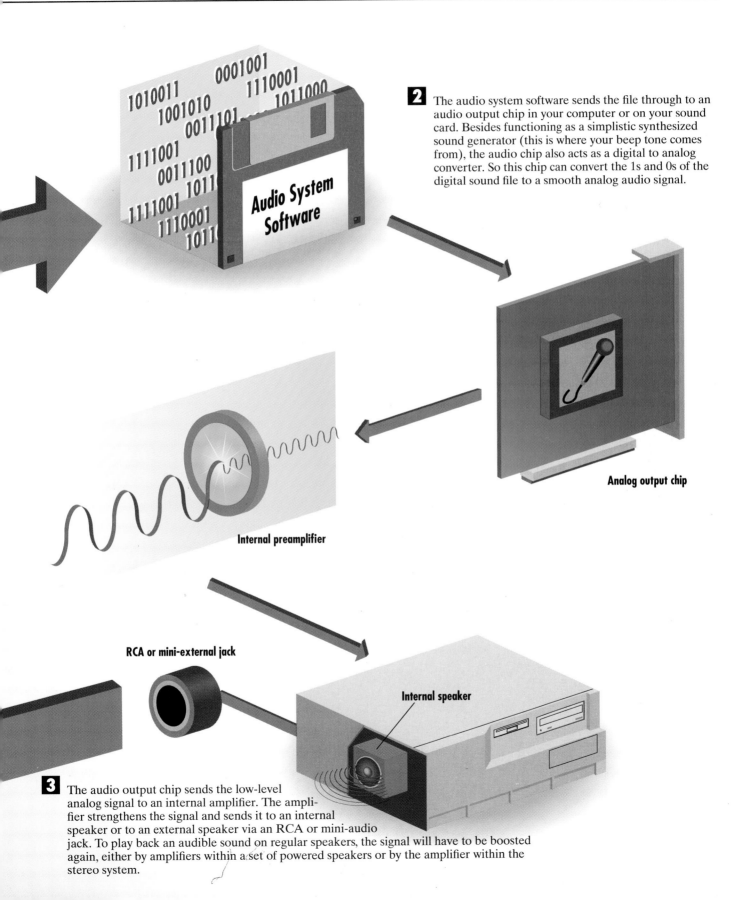

2 The audio system software sends the file through to an audio output chip in your computer or on your sound card. Besides functioning as a simplistic synthesized sound generator (this is where your beep tone comes from), the audio chip also acts as a digital to analog converter. So this chip can convert the 1s and 0s of the digital sound file to a smooth analog audio signal.

Audio System Software

Analog output chip

Internal preamplifier

RCA or mini-external jack

Internal speaker

3 The audio output chip sends the low-level analog signal to an internal amplifier. The amplifier strengthens the signal and sends it to an internal speaker or to an external speaker via an RCA or mini-audio jack. To play back an audible sound on regular speakers, the signal will have to be boosted again, either by amplifiers within a set of powered speakers or by the amplifier within the stereo system.

Understanding Digital Signal Processing

Digital signal processing (DSP) chips are designed to handle a variety of intensive computing tasks. Because these chips are so multifunctional, several computer companies such as Apple, Silicon Graphics, and Atari are using chips such as the Motorola 56001 DSP chip inside some of their computers.

Digital Signal Processing (DSP) Chip

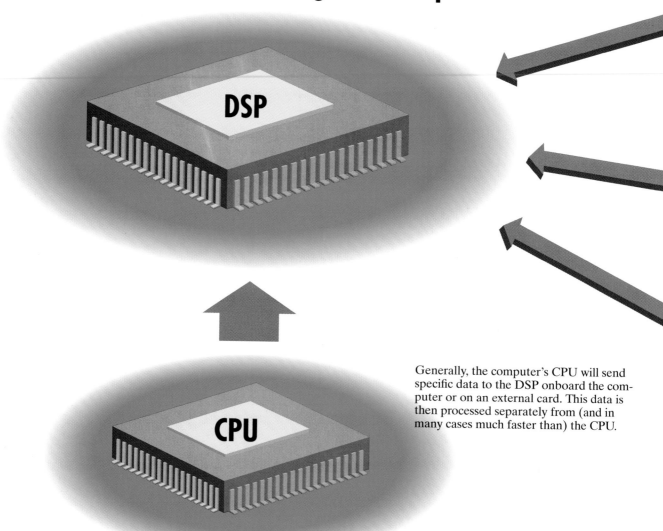

Generally, the computer's CPU will send specific data to the DSP onboard the computer or on an external card. This data is then processed separately from (and in many cases much faster than) the CPU.

DSP chips can dramatically speed up graphics processing. For example, Adobe Photoshop, a popular Mac and Windows program for manipulating photorealistic images, can use a DSP to speed up its functions. Rotating or sharpening an image takes a fraction of the time when a DSP processor is used with Photoshop.

Digital video programs can use DSP to increase their processing speed and play back high-quality digital audio. The Media Suite Pro, a nonlinear editing system from Avid Technology, uses the DSP onboard the Digidesign Audio Media II board bundled with the system to provide CD-quality audio with full-motion video.

Audio playback is just one of the ways DSP chips can improve audio processing. Several manufacturers, such as Digidesign and Lexicon, are creating DSP products that can add reverb, mix levels, and send signals, all within the digital domain. Because the signals stay in the digital domain, their audio fidelity has the potential to be far superior to normal analog products.

Digital Audio in Music Education

If you've ever heard anyone sing "do, re, me, fa, so, la, ti, do," then you've heard someone practicing *Solfeggio* or *sight singing*. The benefits of sight singing are far reaching; from faster sight reading to better control of intonation (how sharp or flat you are). However, most musicians agree that sight singing is one of the most difficult skills that they had to learn. Claire from Opcode Systems is an extraordinary program that uses digital audio to help ease the pain of learning sight singing. Claire uses the built-in digital audio playback and recording capabilities in most Macs to teach sight singing.

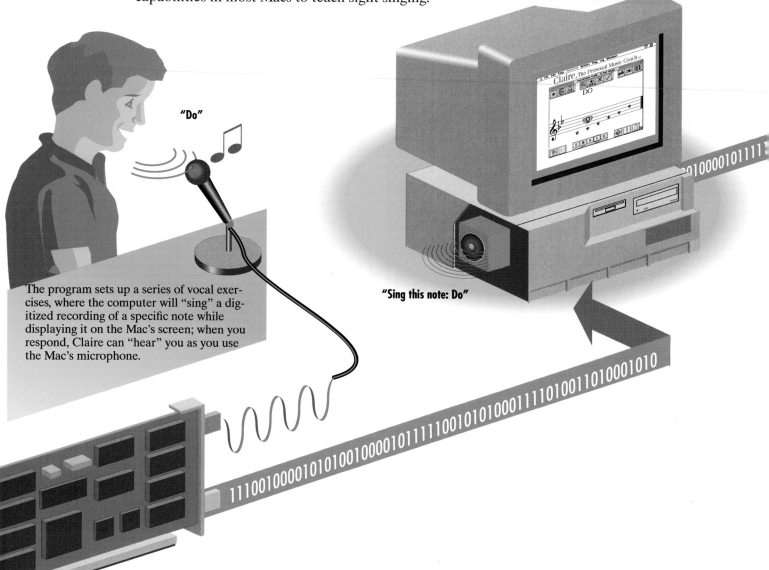

"Do"

The program sets up a series of vocal exercises, where the computer will "sing" a digitized recording of a specific note while displaying it on the Mac's screen; when you respond, Claire can "hear" you as you use the Mac's microphone.

"Sing this note: Do"

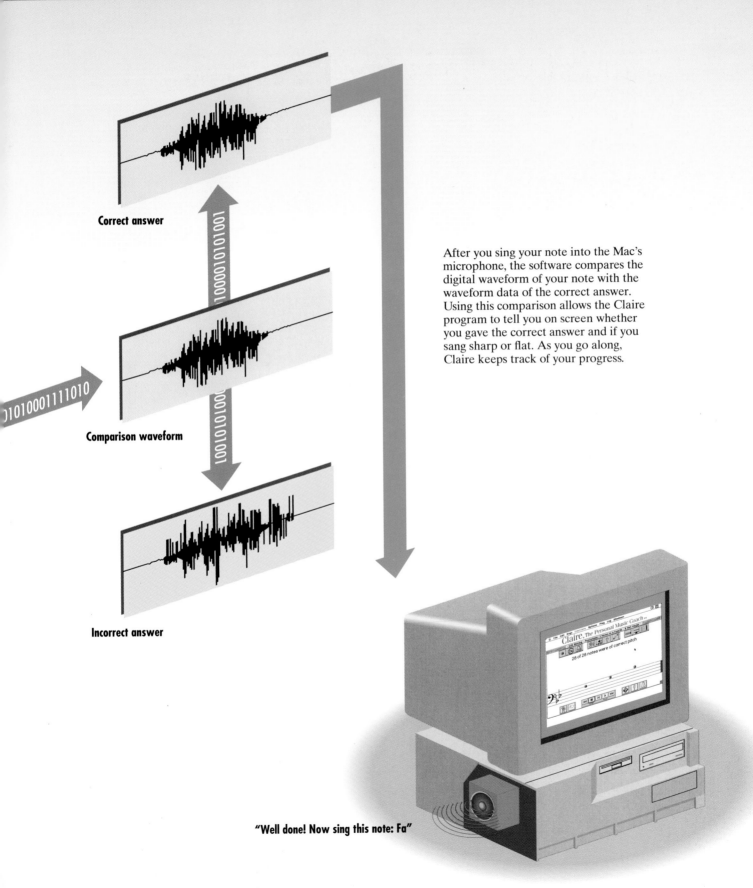

Correct answer

Comparison waveform

Incorrect answer

After you sing your note into the Mac's microphone, the software compares the digital waveform of your note with the waveform data of the correct answer. Using this comparison allows the Claire program to tell you on screen whether you gave the correct answer and if you sang sharp or flat. As you go along, Claire keeps track of your progress.

"Well done! Now sing this note: Fa"

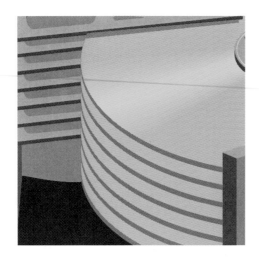

CHAPTER
9

Digital Audio Editing

F YOU'VE EVER had to write on a manual or electric typewriter, you know that it is a pain; if you wanted to make any changes or corrections later on, you had to start from scratch. Now word processors let you cut and paste new material, make corrections, and save multiple versions of document without having to retype everything. Digital audio editing has revolutionized the way producers, engineers, and musicians work with sound in the same way that word processors have changed how we write.

In the early days of audio, engineers would use razor blades and specially designed metal cutting blocks to edit audio tape. With a lot of practice, you could eventually trim edit segments to within a few dozen milliseconds of where you wanted—if your razor was sharp and your hands steady. After you made your cut, you would splice the two sections of audio tape together, hoping that the splice didn't create an audible pop once it went over the playback heads on the reel-to-reel tape recorder. Needless to say, this was a very time-consuming process.

Today's technology allows you to make an unlimited number of changes on your computer's hard disk with incredible accuracy. Instead of being accurate to a few dozen milliseconds, you can edit a 16-bit, CD-quality digital sound to $\frac{1}{44,100}$ of a second; this is the equivalent of changing not just a photograph, but each individual dot within the picture. With this kind of accuracy, engineers can tighten up interviews, piece together multiple versions of vocal solos, or even edit out a single bad note in the middle of a blazing guitar solo.

Editing digital audio from a hard disk has another big advantage: random access. Instead of waiting for a tape to rewind or fast forward, random access editing allows you to go rapidly to any spot in a song. This is because a computer's hard disk is constantly spinning. When you need a particular piece of data, the read/write head of the hard disk moves to that section of the hard disk platter: Imagine a record player that spins incredibly fast, with a needle that plays back data instead of music. The difference here is that a hard disk can read or move over to digital audio files a lot faster than a record player can; in fact, some hard disks can access data as quickly as 13 milliseconds or less.

A variety of programs are available for editing digital audio on personal computers. While there are several editing packages on the PC platform, such as The Turtle Beach 65K hardware software system from Turtle Beach Systems, audio editing software started on the Apple Macintosh platform. Two of the most popular digital audio editing packages available on the Macintosh are Sound Designer II from Digidesign and DECK from OSC. Sound Designer II is designed for use with Digidesign professional digital audio hardware; DECK is a lower-cost package that can work with a variety of hardware boards and the onboard digital processing of the AV series Macintosh computers.

How Digital Audio Editing Works

In traditional audio editing, you can't easily make changes after you've recorded a sound to tape. If you try to add in a new sound, everything after that sound is erased. Conversely, if you erase a bad note, you'll leave a blank spot on the tape. While you can edit tapes using razor blades and adhesive splicing tape, it doesn't have the accuracy of digital audio editing.

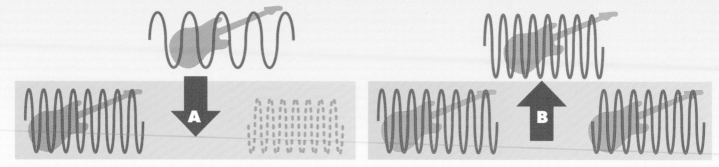

Traditional Audio Editing

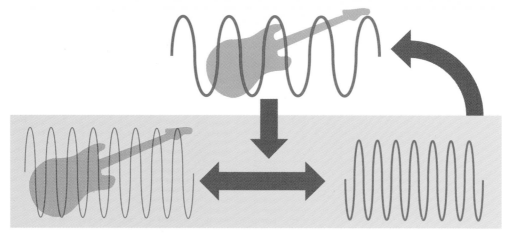

Digital Audio Editing — Digital audio editing lets you cut and paste audio segments together with incredible accuracy in any order you like. Moving a segment from the end of your song over to the middle is not a problem; just pick a spot to insert the new material. After you paste in the new sound, the old material is simply pushed to the end of the new material, or replaced—it's your choice.

To hear an example of digital audio editing, listen to track 4 on the audio CD. Also, check out track 6 for an example of how professional sound designer Alan Howarth puts together sound effects for motion pictures.

Creating Digital Movie Sound Effects

Sound effects often contain dozens of sounds layered on top of each other; this gives the sound effect more depth and makes the action bigger than life. As the playback systems in theaters improve, sound designers are using digital technology to improve fidelity and quality. Here's an example of how sound designers work with digital audio in preparing sound effects.

1 Initially, a sound effects designer often goes out into the field with a professional microphone and records a variety of sounds to be combined later on.

2 To maintain the highest fidelity possible, these sounds are recorded directly to DAT (digital audio tape).

3 Using a digital-to-digital connection on a high-end sound board, the sounds from the DAT are transferred directly to a computer hard disk.

4 Once the data is on the hard disk, the designer uses digital audio editing software, such as Digidesign's Sound Designer (shown here), to layer multiple sounds to create the final sound effect.

5 Finally, the digital sound effect is synchronized to the picture and mixed with the music and dialogue, a process called *audio layback*.

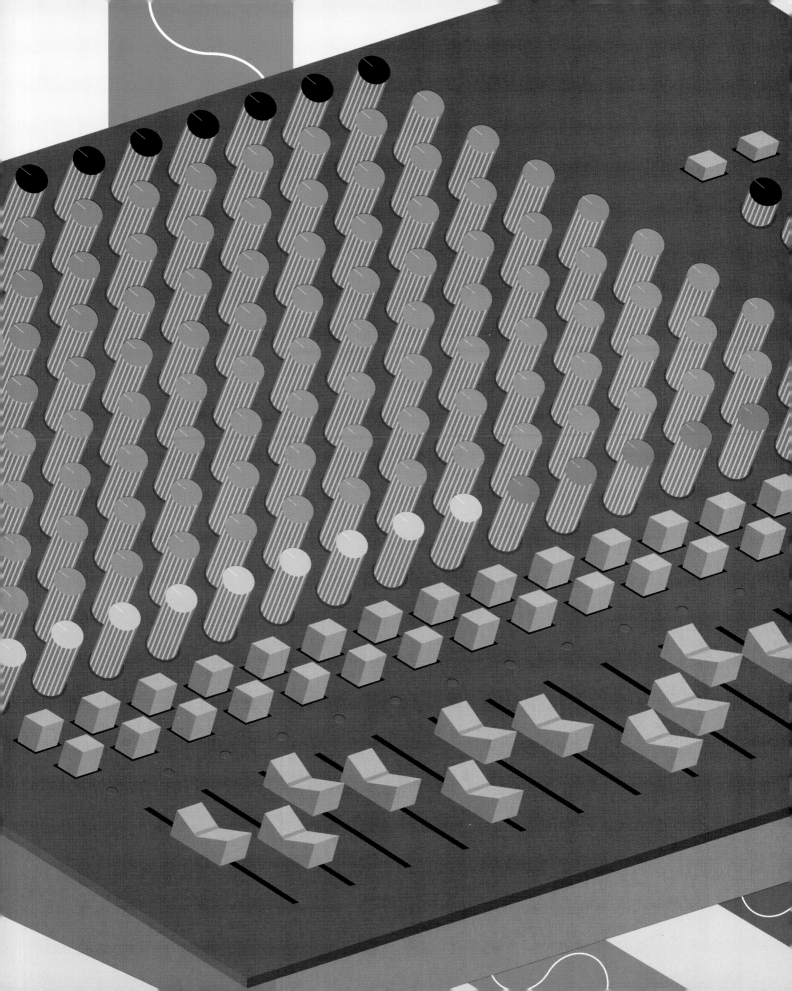

UNDERSTANDING MIDI

4

CONTENTS

I

F YOU WALK into a music or computer store, you might find the variety of MIDI equipment and software available a bit intimidating. There are dozens of different MIDI software programs, MIDI keyboards, MIDI controlled effect units—the list seems unending. If you are like most people, making music with MIDI seems too expensive or complicated to get involved with. However, don't let the techno-babble of the different products deter you, because MIDI is one of the few truly affordable and flexible technologies around.

A simple setup consists of four basic components: a personal computer with MIDI software; a MIDI interface (to send MIDI data in and out of the computer's serial port); a MIDI keyboard or MIDI sound module; and something to output the keyboard's sound, such as powered speakers or a home stereo system. It doesn't matter whether your keyboard costs $5,000 or $500; generally, as long as it has a MIDI in and out port, it will do the job. If you want a better keyboard later on, you can swap your old keyboard for a brand new one; or better yet, just add it to your system. This will give you more notes and an additional keyboard to play parts back on.

You don't need to buy a powerful personal computer to work with MIDI; the small size and the relatively slow data bandwidth of MIDI files allow you to use the most basic computers on the market to make MIDI music. So don't let your old Mac Plus or 386-based PC stop you from getting involved with MIDI; you probably have more than enough machine to get started. While you may not be able to work with all the latest software, chances are you'll find several MIDI software packages that will still work on your machine.

Moreover, you don't have to invest in expensive hardware to make music with MIDI. If you are a musician, but can't afford a full blown professional MIDI setup, don't worry; just buy as much as you can afford. You can use your one MIDI keyboard in your basic MIDI setup to play back and record different parts in your songs. This lets you save money by refining parts or trying out new ideas before you go into the recording studio. At the recording studio, you can take your MIDI composition in on a floppy disk and play it back using the recording studio's MIDI gear. Every note that you recorded in your home MIDI setup is still there when you play your MIDI composition back in the recording studio. The difference is that now you can hear what your song sounds like when played back through the recording studio's expensive collection of MIDI hardware.

The next few chapters will take you through the different elements of MIDI. Chapter 10 will give you a basic technical understanding of what MIDI data is and how it works. This section will also give you a better understanding of all the different things you can do within MIDI data.

As I mentioned before, there is a wide variety of MIDI hardware on the market. To help you sort this out, Chapter 11 shows you what the hardware in a typical MIDI setup looks like and gives details on what to look for when putting together your own system.

Chapter 12 breaks all the different MIDI software packages down into three main categories—sequencing, music notation, and music education software. You'll see how these programs work, as well as what you can do with them.

In the first part of this book, I showed you a few examples of how you can use MIDI at home and in professional music production. Clearly MIDI is a worthwhile musical tool, but you might still be confused about how to get started. To help you along, Chapter 13 discusses how to set up a simple MIDI computer system for both Macintosh and Windows personal computers. This should give you enough background information to get started.

CHAPTER 10

How MIDI Works

MIDI IS SIMPLY a communications standard. It was created by electronic musical equipment vendors to define a way for computer music programs, synthesizers, and other electronic equipment to exchange information and control signals. MIDI is not a digital audio technology.

Think of it this way; if digital audio were a tape recording of a person playing a guitar solo, MIDI would be the sheet music for that solo. While the sheet music itself doesn't generate any actual sound, it does define how fast the music is played, which notes are plucked, and how loudly the guitar is strummed.

A big advantage with MIDI is the comparatively low amount of data that you need to send to and store in your computer. A digital audio file that contains one minute of stereo music takes up about 10 megabytes (or about seven floppy disks worth) of storage space. However, a one-minute MIDI music file only takes up about 8 kilobytes, so you could fit about 175 MIDI tunes on just one floppy disk! This also means that the amount of data you need to send between your computer and your MIDI instruments is very low, so even the lowest model of computer can generally play and record MIDI files.

Perhaps the easiest way to understand how MIDI works is to look at the MIDI message, which is the data you send from one MIDI device to another. The MIDI message contains two distinct types of information: status messages and data messages. A *status message* describes a particular function, such as playing a note or bending the pitch of a sound, while a *data message* describes which note you've played or how far you've bent the note.

When you play a note on a keyboard of a MIDI synthesizer, this generates a MIDI message composed of both status and data messages. The first part of this message contains a status message that describes what it is you're doing; in this case, you are creating a *note on event*, which is a status message that says you are pressing down on a key. This message also describes the MIDI channel of the status message, which is an important part of MIDI.

A *MIDI channel* is a status message describing the destination of the MIDI information. The packets of MIDI data in a MIDI message can be sent to any one of 16 different MIDI channels.

Because each status message includes MIDI channel identification, you can send individual pieces of equipment separate messages along the same MIDI cable. In his excellent book *MIDI for Musicians,* Craig Anderton provides a good analogy to describe how MIDI channels work. He compares them to sorting letters by zip code. As each letter goes through the sorting machine, it is dumped into individual piles according to its zip code destination. MIDI works the same way; messages sent to a specific MIDI channel number are delivered only to the keyboard or MIDI device set to the same channel number. Finally, in most cases, the status message is followed by two data messages. For example, the note on status message would be followed by data on what note was turned on and how hard the note was struck.

MIDI messages include several status types. For example, besides note on and note off (which describes taking your finger off a keyboard), there is also aftertouch, which describes the amount of pressure you exert on the keyboard after you've initially pressed down on a key. Some keyboards can trigger new elements of a sound using aftertouch. For example, you could softly hold a chord of a string sound and then use aftertouch to increase the volume of the sound by pressing down harder on the keys. We'll talk more about velocity and aftertouch in the next chapter.

Pitch bend and program change are two important status messages. *Pitch bend* describes—you guessed it—bending a note up or down in pitch. You usually do this by moving a small wheel alongside a keyboard, where pushing the wheel up or pulling it down will raise or lower the pitch of the keyboard's sound. Most keyboards contain a variety of sounds, which have numbered presets so you can bring them up by entering that number on the keyboard. The *program change* message selects a particular preset number on a MIDI device, such as a keyboard. For example, you could have a saxophone sound on preset number 6, but want to change it to that killer trumpet sound that you have in preset number 26; using a program change message allows you to change the sound automatically.

When you have to gradually change a specific parameter, such as how much vibrato you want to add to a saxophone over a period of time using a modulation wheel, continuous controller messages are ideal. You can send MIDI data to any one of 128 different continuous controllers, which can range from a keyboard's sustain pedal to a volume control slider or a specific knob turning on the keyboard's main panel. For example, by decreasing the value of MIDI controller number 7, you turn down the master volume of a device.

There are also systemwide status messages to control your entire MIDI setup. For example, if your keyboard gets just the note on message, but not the note off, the note in question will continue to play whether you want it to or not. When a note gets "stuck" like this, it's bad; when several notes get stuck on more than one MIDI instrument, it's absolutely maddening. If the equipment that you are using supports it, you can stop this noise instantly by sending out an All Notes Off command from your keyboard or computer. The All Notes Off status message is kind of a MIDI panic button that tells all the MIDI machines in your system to stop playing whatever notes they are hanging onto.

Systemwide status messages are common to all MIDI instruments; *system exclusive* status messages are designed to send specific data to and from a particular manufacturer's machine. Using system exclusive messages you could send the parameters of different sounds from one synthesizer to another—as long as they are the same model and from the same manufacturer. This is because each system exclusive message contains a manufacturer's identification number; your equipment will only respond to the system exclusive data if it uses this number.

As you can see, there is a lot of data contained within MIDI messages, which is why MIDI is such a powerful music communications standard. Now here's the bad news; a MIDI instrument doesn't have to respond to all of these commands to be considered a MIDI instrument. We'll discuss this in more detail in the next chapter, but it's something you need to know now. If you want to build a MIDI system, you'll still need to spend some time going over each piece of hardware's data sheets to be sure that you are getting the right piece of gear. The next few chapters will show you which parts of the MIDI message apply particularly to MIDI hardware, as well as what you'll need to keep in mind as you create your own MIDI system.

How a MIDI Message Works

The beauty of MIDI is that it can send many types of messages. For example, as you play a keyboard, MIDI messages describe which notes you play, the dynamics of your playing, whether you applied pressure to a key after it was pressed down (called aftertouch), sustain pedal movement, and much more.

MIDI messages are extremely compact and travel serially (one piece of data after another) to the computer. While parallel data transmission (where several pieces of data are all sent at the same time) is much faster, the designers of the MIDI specification decided to use serial transmission because it was less expensive. Still, MIDI's serial transmission rate is higher than what you use with typical personal computer serial ports.

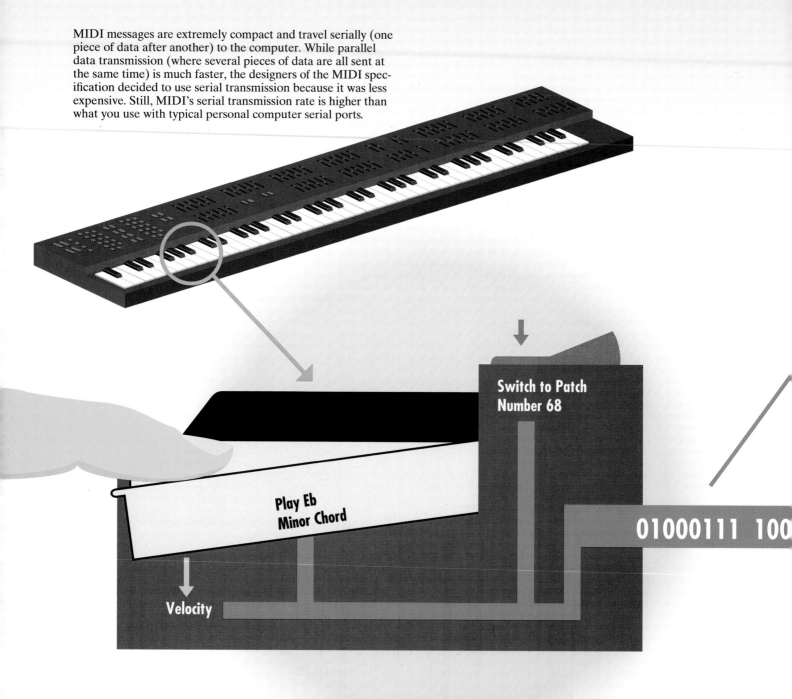

Switch to Patch
Number 68

Play Eb
Minor Chord

Velocity

01000111 100

MIDI data byte

0 1 0 1 1 0 1 0

Start bit   **Stop bit**

A MIDI data byte with a start and stop bit at the beginning and end of the byte is used to aid in decoding the serial MIDI message. The MIDI interface discards these start and stop bits as soon as each command is reassembled.

At the computer, the serial data stream is reassembled into MIDI commands that the computer can record, change, and manipulate. Because you can send so much information from your MIDI instrument, your computer can occasionally get flooded with too much data. This results in a problem called MIDI choke. Using a more sophisticated MIDI interface that can filter out MIDI data to and from your MIDI hardware can solve this problem.

100 00101010 100111

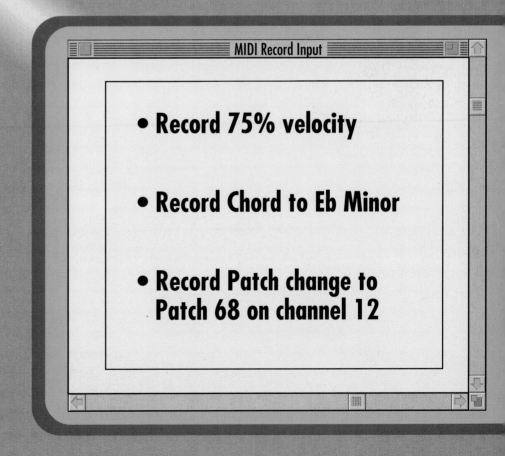

MIDI Record Input

- **Record 75% velocity**

- **Record Chord to Eb Minor**

- **Record Patch change to Patch 68 on channel 12**

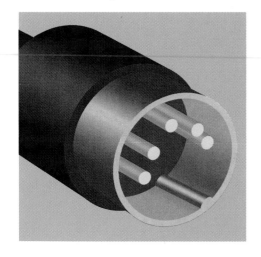

Understanding MIDI Hardware

MIDI HARDWARE IS a bit of a paradox. MIDI was originally designed to solve incompatibilities between different electronic music instruments by defining a standard format of control data and a universal cable system. In this way, a musician could play just one keyboard but have it control many different synthesizers or sound generators at one time. This was a major breakthrough in standardization and cooperation between competing music vendors, and today virtually every electronic instrument—from department store keyboards to professional digital synthesizers—is a MIDI-compatible instrument.

However, the definition of a "MIDI instrument" can vary from vendor to vendor. The most important thing to keep in mind when you look at MIDI equipment is that an instrument doesn't have to implement all aspects of the MIDI specification to be a MIDI instrument.

Some low-cost consumer MIDI equipment may respond to basic MIDI messages (such as note on or off), but it may not respond to program change, pitch bend, or other important MIDI messages. Ultimately it's up to you to find out just how much or how little information a piece of MIDI hardware can respond to. One good way to find out the MIDI capabilities of an instrument is to look at the instrument's MIDI implementation chart, which is usually in the back of the owner's manual. This will outline the kinds of MIDI messages the instrument can send and receive.

There are a few things you should look for when evaluating MIDI hardware. You'll need to look for a MIDI interface, which is the crucial link between your personal computer and your MIDI equipment. The MIDI interface reroutes the digital data coming from the MIDI cable into a format that can be sent to the computer through a serial cable. The computer usually accesses the MIDI data through the serial port, which is normally used for a printer or modem.

As with most MIDI equipment, there is a wide range of prices and features in MIDI interfaces. At the low end, you'll find MIDI interfaces from Music Quest, Key Electronics, Opcode Systems, and others for under $200 that give you one MIDI input port and one or two MIDI output ports. This is fine for a basic system where you only have a few devices hooked up to your system, such as a keyboard and a sound module. At the high end, you can pay anywhere from $600 to $1,300 for a MIDI interface that offers more MIDI output channels, more synchronization capabilities, and enough muscle to handle any professional MIDI system. For example, you can buy the Opcode Systems Studio 5LX for $1,295. It has 15 MIDI input and 15 MIDI output ports, connects to both serial ports on your computer, and can send MIDI data to any of 240 separate MIDI channels!

However, if you don't want to use a keyboard, but just want to play back MIDI files from your computer, you may not need a MIDI interface. Some sound modules, such as the Roland SC-50 Sound Canvas or the Yamaha TG-100, have a built-in MIDI interface, so you can connect them directly to your computer's serial port. Also, several of the sound boards for Windows-based personal computers already have a simple MIDI output port built-in.

MIDI keyboards vary widely in features, sound quality, and price; to try and cover individual features for the dozens of different keyboards isn't possible in one book. However, there are a few things that you should look for in your MIDI keyboard.

First, check whether it can respond to both Omni and Poly mode MIDI messages. In Omni mode, the keyboard will respond to all MIDI information coming in, regardless of what MIDI channel it was set for. Poly mode only responds to MIDI information set for a specific instrument. Poly mode is vital if you plan on using more than one MIDI instrument in your setup, because without it you can't assign individual MIDI channels to each instrument. If you send all of your piano parts to MIDI channel 9 of one keyboard, and the bass guitar to another keyboard on channel 5, unless they can do Poly mode, they will both play back the MIDI data intended for the other keyboard.

If you only have the budget for one keyboard, make sure that it is multi-timbral, meaning that it can play back more than one sound simultaneously and that you can assign a separate MIDI channel to each sound. Using a multi-timbral keyboard, you could assign a bass and drum parts to different channels on the same multi-timbral keyboard, and still play along.

One of the main limitations on the number of parts you can play on a multi-timbral keyboard is the number of voices on the keyboard, or the keyboard's polyphony. *Polyphony* simply means the number of notes that you can play at one time. Most keyboards have at least eight voices, so you can play up to eight notes at one time; or you could have eight different sounds play one note at a time. Look for a multi-timbral keyboard with at least 16-voice polyphony; because the more voices you have, the more parts you can try out. Chances are you'll run out of voices faster than you'd think. Play a single piano triad (a chord made up of three notes), and you've already used up three voices: add a bass guitar part, a lead guitar part, and a drum kit (bass, snare, and high-hat cymbal), and you will use up another five voices.

The kind of MIDI data your keyboard can send is just as important as what it can receive. Some MIDI keyboards send velocity and aftertouch information in addition to note on and off information. Remember, velocity information describes how hard you hit the keys, while aftertouch describes how hard you press down on a key after hitting it. A MIDI keyboard with velocity can make a major difference in how naturally a sound plays back when you hit the keys. Aftertouch isn't in most consumer-level MIDI keyboards, and takes some getting used to; however, it can make a major difference in how expressively you can play your keyboard.

MIDI controller keyboards are another alternative that you should be aware of when shopping for MIDI equipment. A MIDI controller keyboard doesn't usually have any on-board sounds, but can send MIDI note data, including patch change information, velocity, and aftertouch. The MIDI controller is generally used in conjunction with a MIDI sound module.

MIDI sound modules are nothing more than synthesizers without a keyboard; they have all the same sound generation hardware, but require some type of MIDI controller in order to play sounds. MIDI sound modules are a great way to add sounds and voices to your MIDI system because MIDI sound modules are generally much more affordable than MIDI synthesizers with keyboards. MIDI sound modules also are great if you don't have much space for your MIDI system; four MIDI modules take up about as much room as two VCRs stacked on top of each other.

The variety of MIDI modules is somewhat bewildering. The reason for the wide range in MIDI sound modules is the quality of sound and the range of features in a module. Some modules are simple playback modules with limited polyphony, while the more expensive modules are duplicates of professional keyboards. At the low end, you can expect to pay around $350 for a simple MIDI sound module, while professional MIDI sound modules from companies such as Roland, Emu Systems, and Ensoniq can list for $2,000.

General MIDI is another feature that you should keep an eye out for when looking for either a MIDI keyboard or sound module. *General MIDI* is a vendor-sponsored standard that defines specific features and capabilities for MIDI instruments. General MIDI instruments have at least 24 voices of polyphony, can respond to all 16 MIDI channels, are multi-timbral, and can accept a variety of MIDI controller messages. General MIDI also organizes all the different instrument sounds in a keyboard or module into a universal instruments set. General MIDI allows you to play back a MIDI file with approximately the same sounds that the file was originally created with; in other words, the General MIDI specification keeps the instrument sounds and playback features consistent between General MIDI instruments. This is a boon for playing back prerecorded MIDI files, where you can quickly adjust the music to fit a new tempo or key.

When you do finally decide to take the plunge and buy some MIDI gear, be sure to take as much time as you need in music stores trying out individual pieces of equipment. Investing in MIDI equipment can be an expensive venture, and you want to do it right the first time. While you are in a music store, don't be afraid to lean on the experience of the music store salespeople; they are there to help you. The amount of questions you ask about a particular piece of gear and the amount time you spend testing it will make a huge difference after you've made your purchase. If the salesperson isn't willing to let you take your time or answer your questions, say thanks, but no thanks; if they won't give you the attention you need, they aren't worthy of your business. Good salespeople in music stores not only want to sell you gear, they also want you to be happy with what you buy; that way you'll come back for more.

How MIDI Hardware Works

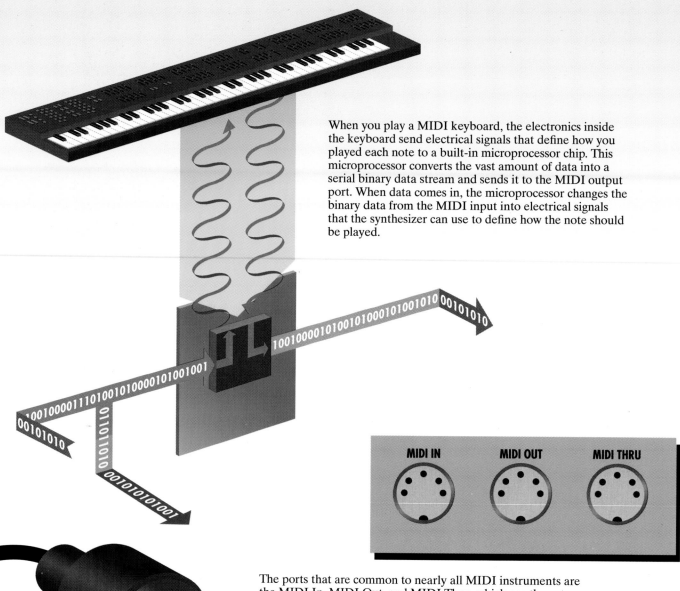

When you play a MIDI keyboard, the electronics inside the keyboard send electrical signals that define how you played each note to a built-in microprocessor chip. This microprocessor converts the vast amount of data into a serial binary data stream and sends it to the MIDI output port. When data comes in, the microprocessor changes the binary data from the MIDI input into electrical signals that the synthesizer can use to define how the note should be played.

The ports that are common to nearly all MIDI instruments are the MIDI In, MIDI Out, and MIDI Thru, which are the gateways for different devices to talk to each other. The *MIDI In* port receives data from other devices; the *MIDI Out* sends MIDI data to other keyboards or devices; and the *MIDI Thru* port simply routes a copy of the MIDI In data directly to another device, by-passing the data sent from the keyboard's MIDI Out port. The 5-pin DIN or MIDI cable can both send and receive MIDI data: Two pins are used to send the MIDI data; one pin is a ground, and the two remaining pins are reserved for possible future enhancements to the MIDI specification.

There is a vast number of MIDI setups for multimedia production: However, a basic MIDI setup would look something like this. A synthesizer is connected via MIDI to a computer. The computer sends MIDI data via a MIDI interface to other external devices, such as sound modules and digital sound processing units. When the computer sends MIDI data back to the synthesizer and external devices, that data is converted by those devices into sounds or other audio-related functions. The output of the MIDI instruments is sent through an audio mixer, amplified, and then sent out through speakers.

Computer with MIDI software

The most important link between the personal computer and synthesizers is the MIDI interface, which interprets the MIDI data for the computer. The MIDI interface sends MIDI data to the computer via a serial cable, which is usually hooked up to the modem or printer port on a computer. After manipulating the MIDI data, the computer sends the MIDI data back through the serial cable to the MIDI interface. The processed MIDI data is then sent back to the synthesizer's MIDI In connector from the MIDI interface's Out connector.

MIDI interface

MIDI sound modules add extra sounds and the ability to play more notes at one time. Most sound modules, such as the Emu Proteus shown here, are multi-timbral. This means that they can play many different types of sounds at one time.

Sound module

A mixer blends together the analog audio outputs of the keyboard and the tone module, and sends the mixed sound to an amplifier and speakers for monitoring.

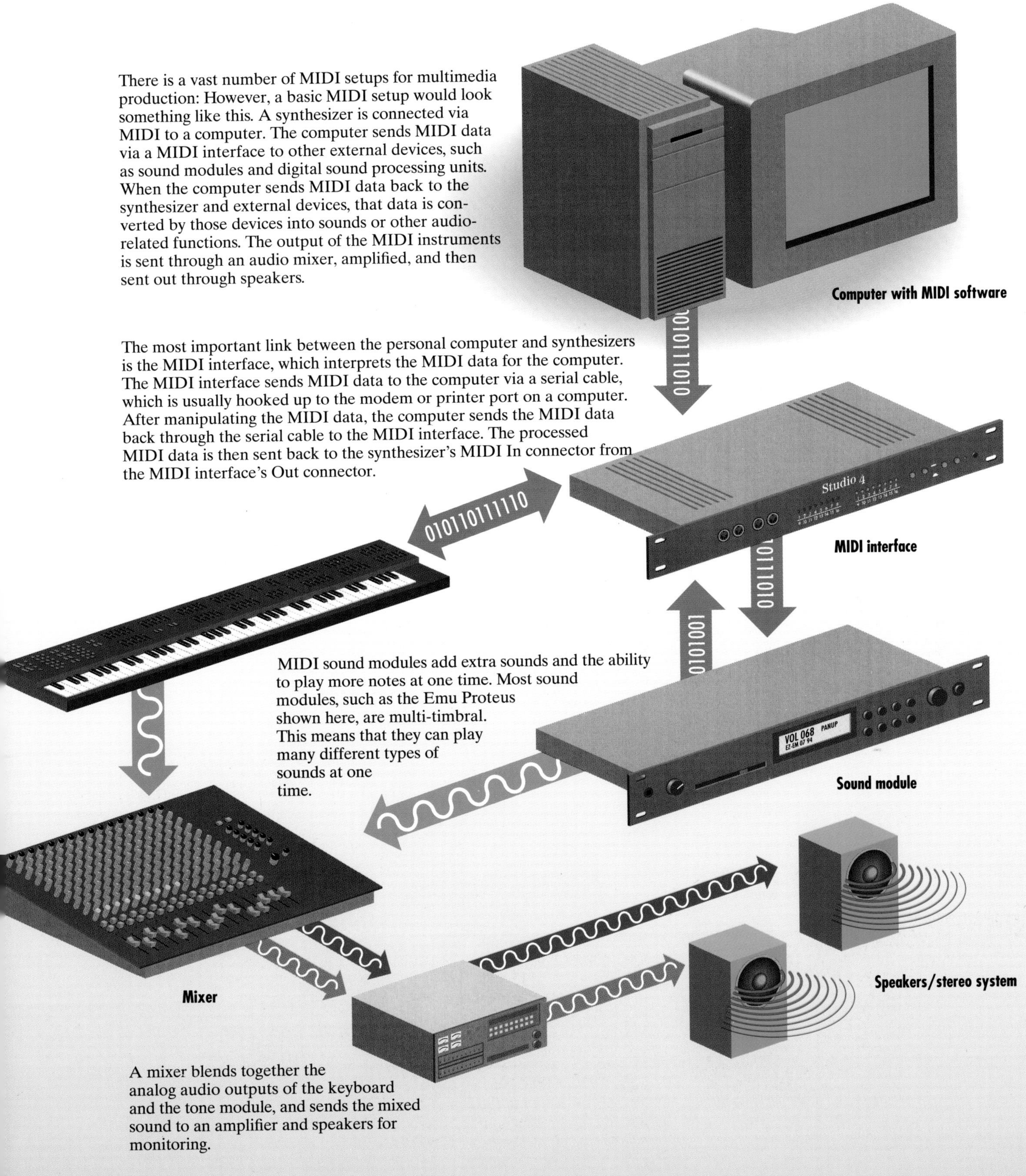

Mixer

Speakers/stereo system

Understanding General MIDI

General MIDI is a vendor specification that defines specific locations for different instrument sounds in the preset memory of synthesizers. This means that a General MIDI file will play back with approximately the same instruments that it was designed for. This is invaluable because keyboard vendors generally put various sounds in different preset locations. Consequently, a MIDI file designed for a piano could be remapped to a trumpet or other sound because there wasn't any way to be consistent. For example, your brass sounds may all be in presets 12 through 16 on your keyboard, but a friend's keyboard has brass sounds assigned to presets 25 through 29. General MIDI solves this problem by organizing all the sounds in a synthesizer or sound module and defining specific requirements for a General MIDI synthesizer. This is a boon for distributing standard MIDI files, adding MIDI music to video games, or just collaborating with another musician.

Piano
1 Acoustic Grand Piano
2 Bright Acoustic Piano
3 Electric Grand Piano
4 Honky-tonk Piano
5 Electric Piano 1
6 Electric Piano 2
7 Harpsichord
8 Clavi

Chromatic Percussion
9 Celesta
10 Glockenspiel
11 Music Box
12 Vibraphone
13 Marimba
14 Xylophone
15 Tubular Bells
16 Dulcimer

Organ
17 Drawbar Organ
18 Percussive Organ
19 Rock Organ
20 Church Organ
21 Reed Organ
22 Accordion
23 Harmonica
24 Tango Accordion

Guitar
25 Acoustic Guitar (nylon)
26 Acoustic Guitar (steel)
27 Electric Guitar (jazz)
28 Electric Guitar (clean)
29 Electric Guitar (muted)
30 Overdriven Guitar
31 Distortion Guitar
32 Guitar Harmonics

Bass
33 Acoustic Bass
34 Electric Bass (finger)
35 Electric Bass (pick)
36 Fretless Bass
37 Slap Bass 1
38 Slap Bass 2
39 Synth Bass 1
40 Synth Bass 2

Strings
41 Violin
42 Viola
43 Cello
44 Contrabass
45 Tremolo Strings
46 Pizzicato Strings
47 Orchestral Harp
48 Timpani

The sounds in a General MIDI synthesizer or sound module are organized into 16 groups, with 8 variations within each group. For example, all the piano sounds are from 1 to 8, with an acoustic piano sound starting at 1. This makes it easier to re-create the right instrument for a specific part of a MIDI sequence.

Ensemble

49	String Ensemble 1
50	String Ensemble 2
51	SynthStrings 1
52	SynthStrings 2
53	Choir Aahs
54	Voice Oohs
55	Synth Voice
56	Orchestra Hit

Brass

57	Trumpet
58	Trombone
59	Tuba
60	Muted Trumpet
61	French Horn
62	Brass Section
63	SynthBrass 1
64	SynthBrass 2

Reed

65	Soprano Sax
66	Alto Sax
67	Tenor Sax
68	Baritone Sax
69	Oboe
70	English Horn
71	Bassoon
72	Clarinet

Pipe

73	Piccolo
74	Flute
75	Recorder
76	Pan Flute
77	Blown Bottle
78	Shakuhachi
79	Whistle
80	Ocarina

Synth Lead

81	Lead 1 (square)
82	Lead 2 (sawtooth)
83	Lead 3 (calliope)
84	Lead 4 (chiff)
85	Lead 5 (charang)
86	Lead 6 (voice)
87	Lead 7 (fifths)
88	Lead 8 (bass + lead)

Synth Pad

89	Pad 1 (new age)
90	Pad 2 (warm)
91	Pad 3 (polysynth)
92	Pad 4 (choir)
93	Pad 5 (bowed)
94	Pad 6 (metallic)
95	Pad 7 (halo)
96	Pad 8 (sweep)

Synth Effects

97	FX 1 (rain)
98	FX 2 (soundtrack)
99	FX 3 (crystal)
100	FX 4 (atmosphere)
101	FX 5 (brightness)
102	FX 6 (goblins)
103	FX 7 (echoes)
104	FX 8 (sci-fi)

Ethnic

105	Sitar
106	Banjo
107	Shamisen
108	Koto
109	Kalimba
110	Bagpipe
111	Fiddle
112	Shanai

Percussive

113	Tinkle Bell
114	Agogo
115	Steel Drums
116	Woodblock
117	Taiko Drum
118	Melodic Drum
119	Synth Drum
120	Reverse Cymbal

Sound Effects

121	Guitar Fret Noise
122	Breath Noise
123	Seashore
124	Bird Tweet
125	Telephone Ring
126	Helicopter
127	Applause
128	Gunshot

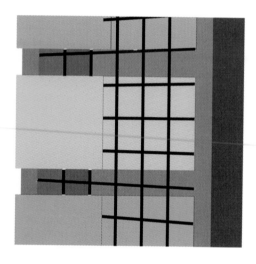

Understanding
MIDI Software

THE KEY COMPONENT of the flexibility of a MIDI system is the wide variety of MIDI software available. No matter what your budget, musical application, or computer platform, chances are there is a MIDI software program available that will meet your needs. Like MIDI hardware, you can buy as complex or simple a MIDI software package as you need and upgrade later on.

Although each MIDI software package is different, they all perform similar tasks; if you understand the various types of MIDI software, you'll be better able to rate the product when you are shopping. There are five categories of MIDI software available: sequencing, music notation, patch editing, music education, and combination programs that contain many or all of these categories.

A sequencer is the most important part of your MIDI system. A *sequencer* is hardware or software that records MIDI data; it is the solid-state equivalent of how a professional studio tape recorder records many channels of sound. Like a multitrack tape recorder, you can record many separate parts into the sequencer; the main difference is that the sequencer only records the MIDI data of your performance, not the sound. Player pianos and music boxes are both based on a type of mechanical sequencer. The roll of paper in the player piano and the metal spindle with raised metal bumps in the music box are similar to sequencer files, in that they can play back music on a hardware device (such as the piano or the music box), but they don't actually contain any sound.

Sequencers, unlike tape decks, are only limited by your hardware's available RAM (random-access memory) and storage capacity. So, you won't have to worry about running out of tape before you've finished your musical masterpiece. Lower-cost hardware-based sequencers that you find in home keyboards are limited by the amount of parts and number of notes they can record. However, the sky is the limit with most computer-based sequencer software; some systems can hold well over 50,000 notes and hundreds of tracks worth of MIDI data.

Once you've recorded the MIDI version of your performance into the sequencer, you can use the sequencer to edit your music with more precision that any audio recording deck. For example, let's say you record a piano part nearly perfectly, but you played a wrong note in the middle of the passage that ruins the track, which distracted you so you played the part after that too softly. If you used a tape recorder, you'd have to go back and rerecord that part—but with a sequencer it's no problem. Most MIDI sequencer software lets you edit each individual note and make global changes (such as setting new tempos) that affect the entire sequence. All you have to do is use the sequencer's editing features to change or delete the bad note, and then adjust the velocity for the next passage.

You can use a sequencer to adjust the tempo, or how fast you play a song. A sequencer also allows you to alter the tempo for each part you record. With a tape recorder you can change the tempo of a song by changing how fast the tape moves past the playback heads. You should also note that altering the speed of the tape will either raise or lower the pitch of the song. However, you can change the tempo of a MIDI file within a sequencer without changing the pitch. Like the player piano roll, a MIDI file is just data, not sound, so when you increase or decrease the tempo, you just change the rate at which the sequencer plays the data back. The song comes out at the same pitch: only the tempo of the music is faster or slower.

Step recording is a feature on sequencers that allows you to record a part one note at a time, so you can record super fast parts that you couldn't ordinarily play. It is not done in real time. For example, let's say you wanted to play a complicated series of triplets so that one measure contains 24 notes. Now imagine trying to play this set of notes with a super fast tempo, and you'll see the advantage of step recording. Alternatively, you could just slow down the tempo of the sequencer to a crawl and record the part.

Music notation software combines elements of a page-layout program with MIDI software so that you can create and print traditional sheet music. You can place notes onto a page by dragging a note onto the score using a mouse, by entering notes from a MIDI keyboard, or by importing a standard MIDI file from your sequencer program. With music notation software, you can create anything from simple sheet music for a song to an orchestral score with all individual parts for a symphony orchestra. Within the program, you can transpose individual parts or entire sections; for vocalists this is a boon, especially if you need to change some music to fit your vocal range.

You'll find that the printed output of music notation software is vastly more readable than music written by hand, but it isn't much faster. Some programs do a fairly good job of transcribing MIDI files, yet they still require you to do a significant amount of cleanup work. To date, even the most sophisticated programs require a lot of work before you can create a score with exactly the right look. However, most music notation packages are great for basic tasks, such as creating songs for a church choir, lead sheets for your band, or individual harmony parts for your vocal group.

The MIDI capabilities within music notation programs are acceptable for checking the accuracy of your notation. However, you'll find that music notation programs are not a good replacement for a dedicated sequencer program.

If you like changing the sounds in your keyboards or sound modules, then you should take a look at patch editing software. Instead of viewing each individual parameter in the tiny LCD of most synthesizers and sound modules, *patch editing* software displays all the instruments' parameters on screen using system exclusive MIDI data. *System exclusive data* is basically a dump of all the information within a MIDI instrument, particularly the details about specific sounds or patches within the instrument. Once in the patch editing program, you can edit sounds, rearrange the order of patches, or just save libraries of your favorite patches. If you plan on regularly changing your sounds, then you should definitely look into one of the different patch editing software packages, including Galaxy from Opcode Systems, Unisyn from Mark of the Unicorn, and Windows-based software from Sound Quest.

If you are a beginning musician, there is a variety of music education software available that takes advantage of MIDI hardware. The Software Toolworks puts out software-only Macintosh and Windows versions of its popular Miracle Piano software, so you can pick the MIDI keyboard you want to use and play along with a variety of exercises and drills. To improve your sight reading skills, there are a variety of ear training programs, such as the Music Lessons program from Mibac for both Mac and Windows, which takes input from a MIDI keyboard or a computer mouse. Music education software is a great way to supplement regular music lessons, because it provides self-paced exercises and documents your progress without any of the pressure of a classroom setting.

Ultimately, finding the right program is a matter of trail and error. While it's impossible to rate each individual program in this book, there are a few general things to keep in mind when you go shopping. In general, low-cost programs will provide you with a good number of sequencing features. More expensive packages, such as Opcode's Vision 2.0 and Mark of the Unicorn's Performer software, will add more control of the MIDI messages in your MIDI system. These are two of the most popular high-end software sequencers on the Mac. They can record and edit note on-and-off messages, as well as adjust every type of MIDI controller message. For example, they can set up your MIDI hardware to receive specific messages from specific cables in your MIDI interface, send and receive patch information, and even simulate a mixing console to control all controller information in real time.

Finally, the most complex program is not necessarily the best program. For the amateur MIDI enthusiast, the number of features within the high-end programs is like hitting a fly with a sledgehammer. Yes, it does get the job done, but the amount of effort it may take you to use the tool may not be worth it. The best thing you can do is try out different programs if possible, to get a feel for how you can work with the program. Of course, pick a complex software package if you like; or if not, just work with a simpler program for now and upgrade to the more advanced program later on. Some companies offer standard and advanced versions of a program, with a reasonable upgrade policy for those who bought the standard version.

How Sequencing Software Works

Sequencers record incoming MIDI data and organize it into discrete parts, or *tracks,* within the sequencer. A track is simply a separate place in which the sequencer puts information, in the same way that a tape recorder keeps sounds separate by putting them on individual channels. Early sequencer programs limited the number of tracks you could use. Now, most sequencer programs provide at least 16 tracks; others offer an unlimited number of tracks to record separate parts.

Each track contains not just note on-and-off information, but also any MIDI messages that are part of the track, including velocity, aftertouch, and all program changes. You can record these MIDI messages when you initially play your part into the sequencer, or add them in after recording using the sequencer editing tools. Sequencer programs, such as Opcode's Studio Vision Pro shown here, have a variety of editing controls to precisely edit each track until it's perfect.

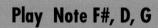

Play Note F#, D, G

Set Tempo to 111 Beats per Note

Increase Mixer Channel 10 Volume to Full

Change Sound Module to Preset #45

When you play back files from the sequencer, all the changes you've made in the program's binary computer code are converted to MIDI data. This MIDI data is sent via the computer's serial port to all MIDI instruments connected to the MIDI interface. One nice feature built into nearly all sequencers is the ability to play back and record MIDI data at the same time: This allows you to hear previously recorded parts while adding a new track.

To hear how sequencers make it easy to create lush, full arrangements of songs, play track 10 on the CD. Track 5 on the CD also contains an example of combining digital audio with MIDI in pop music, featuring an interview with Thomas Dolby.

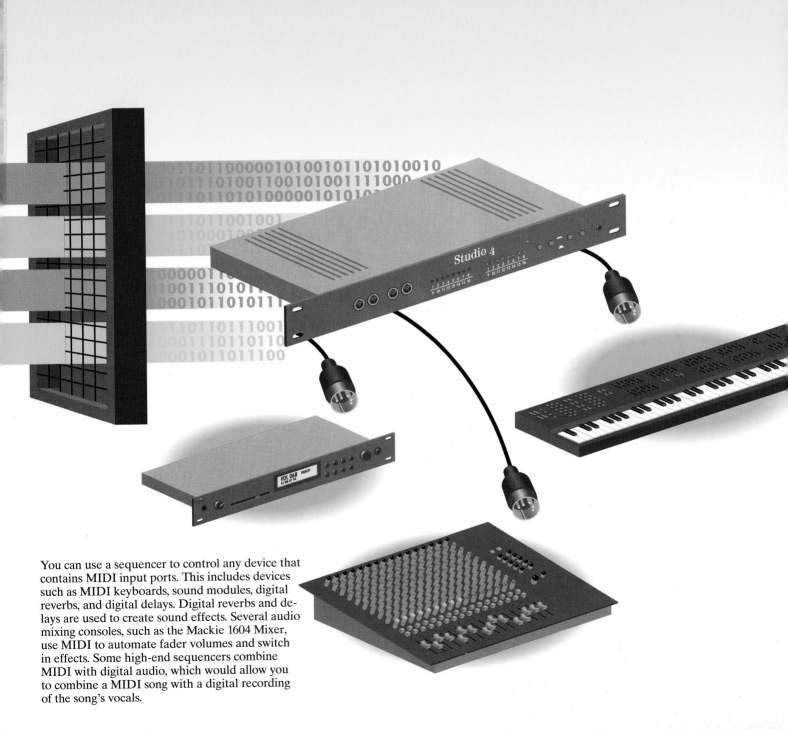

You can use a sequencer to control any device that contains MIDI input ports. This includes devices such as MIDI keyboards, sound modules, digital reverbs, and digital delays. Digital reverbs and delays are used to create sound effects. Several audio mixing consoles, such as the Mackie 1604 Mixer, use MIDI to automate fader volumes and switch in effects. Some high-end sequencers combine MIDI with digital audio, which would allow you to combine a MIDI song with a digital recording of the song's vocals.

How Notation Software Works

Music notation programs are page layout programs: Instead of just using letters, they arrange notes on musical staffs. Some programs, such as Passport Design's Encore program shown here, also allow you to enter music notation using a MIDI keyboard or by importing a standard MIDI file.

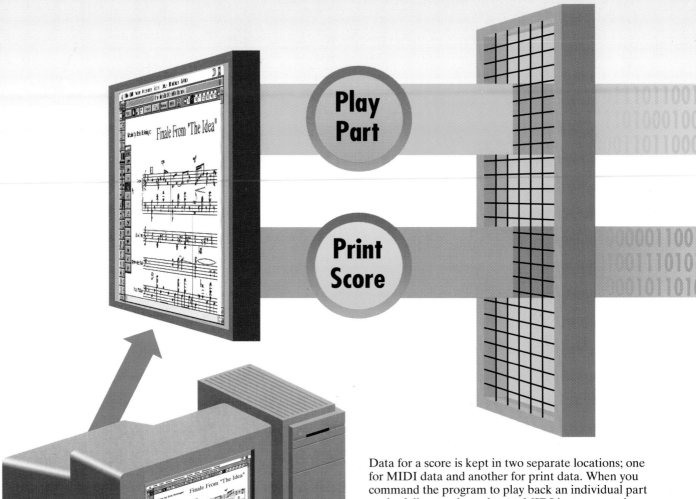

Play Part

Print Score

Data for a score is kept in two separate locations; one for MIDI data and another for print data. When you command the program to play back an individual part or the full score through your MIDI instrument, the program interprets all the graphic data in the score, converts it to MIDI data, and then sends the MIDI data out to each instrument connected to your MIDI system. When you command the program to print a score, the program converts all of the graphic data within the score to a PostScript file for output on a PostScript printer.

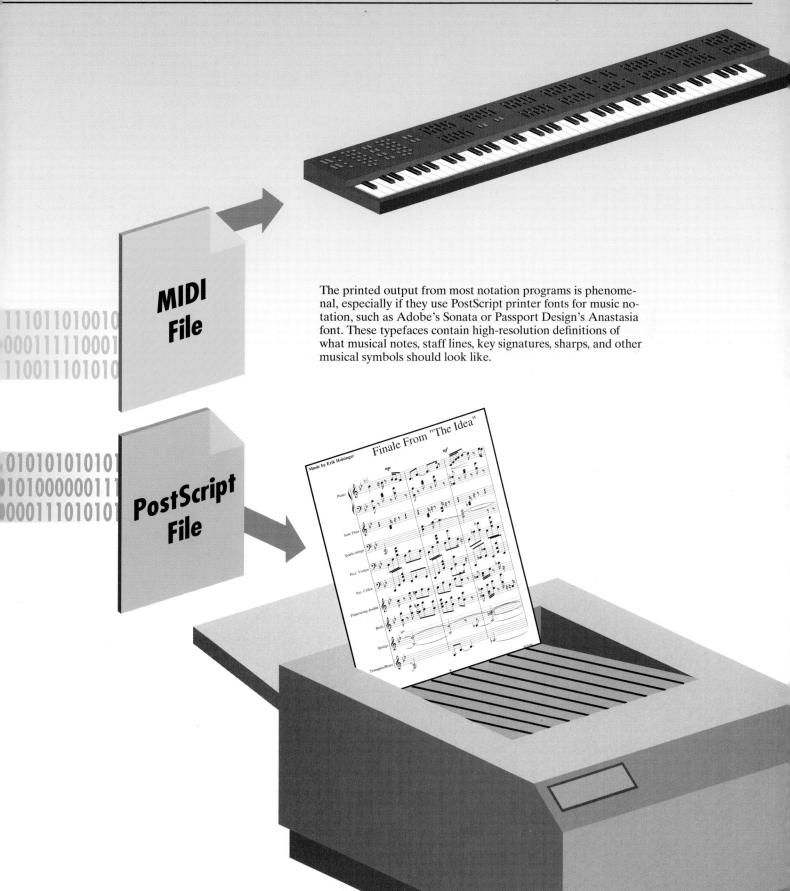

MIDI File

PostScript File

The printed output from most notation programs is phenomenal, especially if they use PostScript printer fonts for music notation, such as Adobe's Sonata or Passport Design's Anastasia font. These typefaces contain high-resolution definitions of what musical notes, staff lines, key signatures, sharps, and other musical symbols should look like.

Finale From "The Idea"

Music by Erik Holsinger

CHAPTER

13

Building Your Own MIDI System

YOU MIGHT FIND shopping for a MIDI system to be a bit confusing. The endless varieties of keyboards, software, and so on can numb even the most courageous shopper. Before you start shopping, the most important thing you need to decide is how you want to use your system. Do you want to improve your music skills, create your own music, or simply play around with MIDI? Once you decide this, you'll find it is easier to work out a budget and to pick the right hardware for your system.

A keyboard (or other MIDI controller) is an essential part of any MIDI setup where your focus is on creating music. Chapter 11 gave you a good idea of some of the features to look for in your main MIDI keyboard. Questions such as how many notes of polyphony does it have, is it multi-timbral, and how well does it implement MIDI are crucial when shopping for a MIDI keyboard. Another important feature is purely subjective, but important in the long run: Do you like how it sounds? Don't buy a keyboard just because it has the specifications that you want; it should also sound good to you. Keyboards are not small purchases, so it's likely that you will own your keyboard for some time.

However, you should buy only what you need right now. Don't spend a lot of time worrying about how you'll get the money to buy a keyboard with features that you may need later on; if you can't afford it, just get what you can. If you need a professional keyboard for a particular project, you can always rent one from some music stores or rent time on one in a recording studio. Renting a more expensive machine makes a lot of sense because you can play back a MIDI sequence that you created at home.

You should also keep in mind that electronic keyboards, like computers, are victims of obsolescence; what is hot now might not be around next year. While some music manufacturers attempt to keep their product lines compatible with earlier models, most of the time these efforts backfire. However, you can take advantage of this obsolescence by getting some great deals on used synths, or by waiting for the price of your dream keyboard to drop, as a keyboard that costs you $3,000 today will cost far less in just a few years. In his book *Vintage Synthesizers*, author Mark Vail points out that some synthesizers that cost over $7,000 in the late 1980s, such as the dual keyboard

Prophet 10 from Sequential Circuits, now have a street price of $500 to $1,200. Although it's not a good idea to wait forever, you can use keyboard obsolescence to buy a perfectly good MIDI keyboard that you couldn't normally afford.

If you want to print out music using music notation software, you should also have access to a PostScript printer. Each of the notation software programs uses a PostScript font designed specifically to output music, such as Adobe's Sonata font. While PostScript rendering programs such as Adobe Systems Adobe Type Manager allow you to print out PostScript files to dot-matrix or ink-jet printers, you won't get great results. If you don't have a Postscript printer, don't worry about it. Just use any other type of printer that is available to do proofs of your musical score, and then take your file to a local copy house or desktop publishing service bureau; there you can rent time on any of their PostScript printers and print out a super high resolution copy of your score.

If you are just interested in using MIDI in conjunction with entertainment software and don't have any use for a keyboard, you should consider buying a sound module or card instead. You should be sure that the card or module is General MIDI compatible. Both sound modules and sound cards are less expensive than a keyboard, and they can also save you the added expense of buying a MIDI interface. For example, both Roland's SC-50 Sound Canvas and Yamaha's TG300 sound module include a built-in MIDI interface, so you can connect either unit directly to the serial port of your Mac or PC. Windows users have an even lower cost alternative when they choose Roland's SCC-1 sound card. This card combines all the sounds of the General MIDI Sound Canvas module with a MIDI interface for under $400.

A number of accessories are also essential, especially MIDI cables you'll need to connect the MIDI hardware in your system. For a keyboard-based system you'll need two cables, one to send MIDI data to the keyboard and one to send MIDI data from the keyboard to the computer. MIDI cables will run you from $5 to $15 depending upon the length of the cable. It's unlikely that you'll find them, but you should avoid buying MIDI cables that are any longer than 50 feet: The MIDI data signal can't operate beyond this range. MIDI cables are generally all usable; the only real difference between one brand and another is in the type of wiring they use, the kind of metal in the connectors, and the amount of shielding. Ultimately you shouldn't try and save money here, as just one MIDI cable can make or break your system.

If you are using more than one keyboard or have a keyboard with several sound modules, you'll also need to invest in a mixer. Mixer prices and features vary widely, with prices staring around $300 for simple four-input mixers to over $800 to $2,000 or more for professional mixers with 16 or more inputs. When investing in a mixer, try to get one that has a few more inputs than you need, as inevitably you'll fill up the extra channels with something; mixers, like nature, abhor a vacuum.

If you are still not sure where to begin, take a look at the software that you would like to use in your system. Researching different software packages is another good way to find out what hardware you'll need. Just go into a music or computer store and look at the MIDI software package; chances are it has a list of the required computer and MIDI hardware needed to run the software. Pay particular attention to the "minimum requirements" section: This will list the bare essentials for your system. Sometimes the software will also have a list of recommendations along with the minimum requirements, such as "2 megabytes of RAM required, 4 megabytes recommended." In this case you should check with the salesperson or the company to know how strongly they recommend the extra hardware; sometimes the additional hardware is essential to make the software more than just barely functional. Generally, the more powerful the program, the more you'll need to worry about the suggested requirements for your hardware.

While the cost of your MIDI hardware can vary widely, the one thing you don't have to wonder about is whether your computer system is powerful enough. Virtually any Mac or PC computer system that has or can add a serial port can run MIDI programs, from your old 286 or 386 PC to the venerable Mac Plus. While more sophisticated and powerful MIDI programs will require more RAM than some of these earlier models can contain, most simple programs require very little hardware.

Deciding whether you need a PowerMac or Pentium computer to improve your Mac or PC MIDI system isn't that much of a consideration. The huge installed base of machines with 386, 486, 68030, and 68040-based machines means that software is plentiful, and support for those programs will continue for a while longer. The PowerMac includes emulation software that allows it to run most System 7-compatible Mac software. However, it is not much faster than a Mac IIci, owing to the speed penalty that is involved in emulating a different operating system. Once applications appear that are written in the PowerMac's native language, you will be able to take advantage of the PowerMac's high-speed operation, but most of this software won't hit the market for another few years. The same situation applies to the Pentium.

While you don't need a very fast computer to run most MIDI software, speed does make a difference in the following areas: screen redraws, operations involving lots of math (such as transposing multiple tracks in a sequence), timing accuracy, and loading files. You should also keep in mind that the new generation of high-power MIDI programs tends to need more and more memory. For example, a stock Mac Plus with 1MB of RAM will simply not run most of today's high-end sequencers.

Here's the bottom line on building your own MIDI system: Don't let an inexpensive computer hold you back from making music because there are may MIDI software packages that will run on it. On the other hand, if you can afford more power, go for it. You'll be glad you did next year when you don't have to trade in your computer! Incidentally, if you can't decide between a 68040 Macintosh and a PowerMac, you can often get a great deal on the 68040 machine and later upgrade it to a PowerMac.

The next few pages will give you an idea of how simple it is to set up a PC or Mac MIDI system. I chose one of hundreds of possible hardware combinations; each system has its own benefits and costs. For example, by using a different keyboard, you could reduce the cost of the system by hundreds of dollars. Still, a MIDI system that you put together yourself is flexible enough to handle most basic MIDI tasks, while still being somewhat affordable. Hopefully your first system will get you off to a good start.

How to Put Together a PC MIDI System

There are several hundred versions of MIDI systems for DOS and Windows users: The equipment here is just one example of a low-cost system. The main keyboard resembles Roland's JV-35, a 16-part multi-timbral general MIDI synthesizer with 24-voice polyphony. This MIDI interface looks like the Music Quest MIDI card with a single MIDI in and out port. The controller software is MusicTime from Passport systems, which combines music notation with sequencer capabilities. The total price of this system is just under $1,700; by swapping different equipment you can reduce or increase the price of this system dramatically.

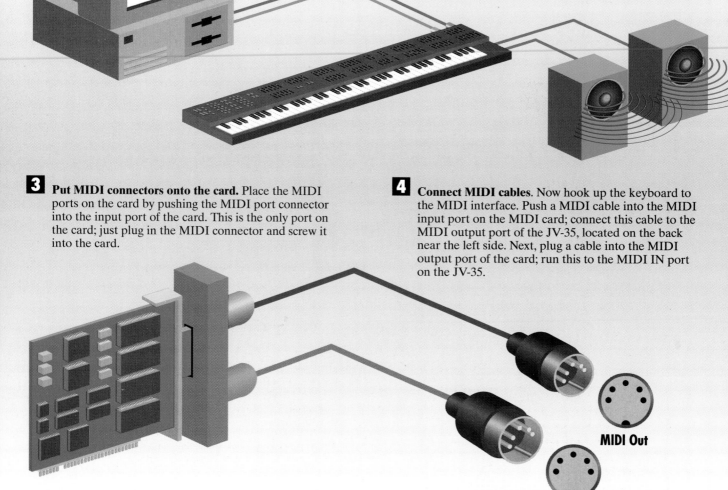

3 **Put MIDI connectors onto the card.** Place the MIDI ports on the card by pushing the MIDI port connector into the input port of the card. This is the only port on the card; just plug in the MIDI connector and screw it into the card.

4 **Connect MIDI cables.** Now hook up the keyboard to the MIDI interface. Push a MIDI cable into the MIDI input port on the MIDI card; connect this cable to the MIDI output port of the JV-35, located on the back near the left side. Next, plug a cable into the MIDI output port of the card; run this to the MIDI IN port on the JV-35.

MIDI Out

MIDI In

1 **Turn off your computer and monitor and then remove its cover.** Be sure everything is turned off before removing the cover. When dealing with anything electrical, be sure to do it away from any liquids—or else you'll get a shocking surprise.

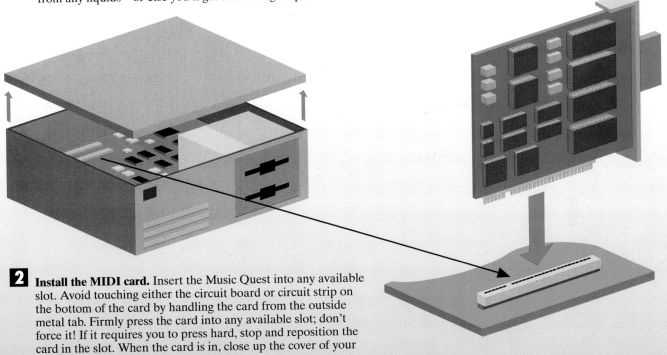

2 **Install the MIDI card.** Insert the Music Quest into any available slot. Avoid touching either the circuit board or circuit strip on the bottom of the card by handling the card from the outside metal tab. Firmly press the card into any available slot; don't force it! If it requires you to press hard, stop and reposition the card in the slot. When the card is in, close up the cover of your computer.

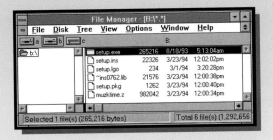

5 **Begin software installation.** Put in the first disc of the MusicTime software and locate the Setup.exe file. This will automatically put the MusicTime application and all required drivers onto your hard drive and into your Windows system file. In Windows just select this file using File Manager, and then hit Run.

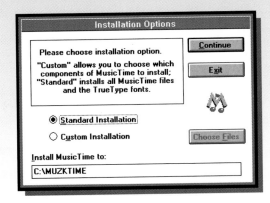

6 **Select software destination.** A screen will come up telling you how much space the installation will take and how much space is available on your hard disk. Pick which hard disk you want to install the software on, and then hit Install. The program will automatically prompt you to put one of the floppy disks into the disk drive. A *prompt* message will come up if the installation was a success. That's it! Now all you need to do is configure your software to match your system.

How to Put Together a Mac MIDI System

There are several hundred versions of MIDI systems for Mac users: The equipment here as just one example of a low-cost system. The main keyboard shown here Roland's JV-35, a 16-part multi-timbral general MIDI synth with 24-voice polyphony. The Music Translator MIDI interface and EZ Vision software come from Opcode as part of its Easy Music Starter Kit. The total price of this system, not including powered speakers, is just under $1,600; by swapping different equipment you can dramatically reduce or increase the price of this system.

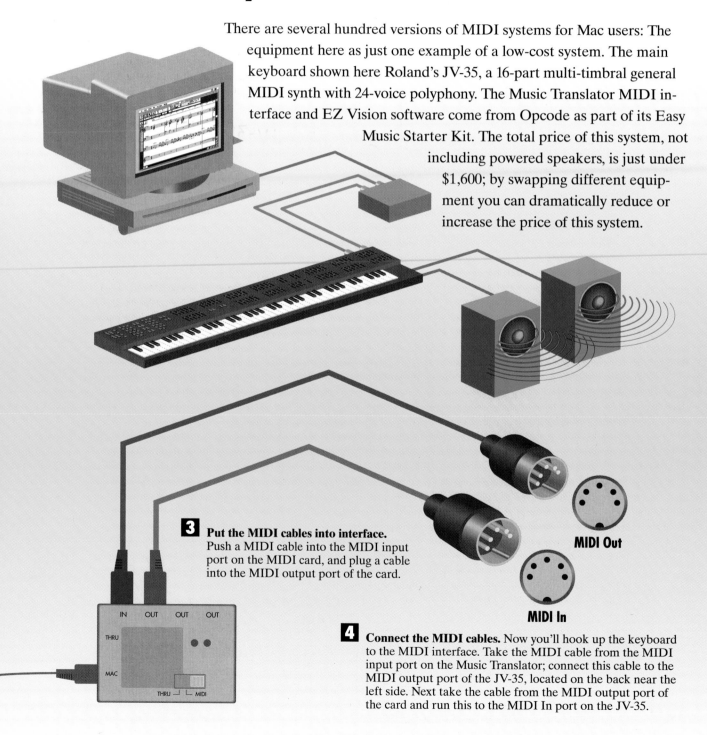

MIDI Out

MIDI In

3 **Put the MIDI cables into interface.** Push a MIDI cable into the MIDI input port on the MIDI card, and plug a cable into the MIDI output port of the card.

4 **Connect the MIDI cables.** Now you'll hook up the keyboard to the MIDI interface. Take the MIDI cable from the MIDI input port on the Music Translator; connect this cable to the MIDI output port of the JV-35, located on the back near the left side. Next take the cable from the MIDI output port of the card and run this to the MIDI In port on the JV-35.

1 **Put the serial cable on the interface.** This cable will connect your interface to your computer. Gently insert this cable into the In port on the side of the interface. Make sure that the slider on the front is set to *MIDI*, otherwise all data will be channeled to the wrong serial port.

2 **Install the MIDI interface.** Insert the serial cable coming from the Music Translator interface into the modem serial port on the back of your Mac. Both serial ports have small icons above them; the printer has one in the shape of a printer, and the modem port has a phone handset above the port. To avoid problems with AppleTalk, Apple's connectivity system software, you should use the modem port rather than the printer port. Firmly press the connector into the port; don't force it! If it requires you to press hard, stop and reposition the connector in the slot.

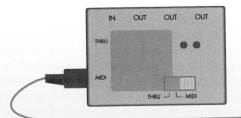

5 **Begin software installation.** Put in the first disk of the EZ Vision software, and double click on the Install Musicshop icon. This will automatically put the Musicshop application and all required system software onto your hard drive and into your system folder.

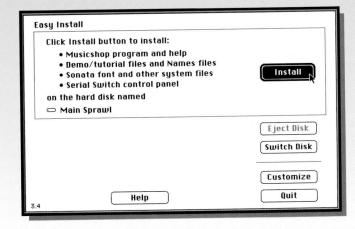

6 **Select software destination.** A screen will come up telling you how much space the installation will take and how much space is available on your hard disk. Pick which hard disk you want to install the software on by clicking on Drive, and then hit Install. The program will automatically prompt you to put one of the floppy disks into the disk drive. When the installation is complete, a message will come up telling you whether it was a success. That's it! Now all you need to do is configure your software to match your system.

SYNTHESIZERS AND MIDI CONTROLLERS

CONTENTS

ELECTRONIC SYNTHESIZERS AND MIDI controllers are the two areas where the marriage of musical and computer technology tends to blend together. On the one hand, if you look inside the cases of today's keyboards you'll find many of the same technologies that are also used to manufacture personal computers. For example, keyboards and computers both rely on sophisticated microprocessors and random access memory (RAM) for trafficking data. On the other hand, anyone who plays a MIDI controller will tell you that they are creating music—not just sending binary MIDI data to keyboards or sound modules. This is in spite of the fact that MIDI controllers do not actually produce any sound.

Nevertheless, when you add a synthesizer to your MIDI system, there are many variables to keep in mind. For instance, you will want access to a sound's basic parameters if you want to change the *attack*, or when the sound plays as you touch a key. If you don't want to fiddle with a sound's parameters, then you'll need to find a keyboard that has all or most of the sounds you'll need already preset in its memory. Musicians who perform live will need easy access to the switching sounds, as well as to other performance controls. With all these different requirements, it's impossible for any vendor to make an electronic keyboard that will fit everyone's needs; however, with a bit of shopping you should find a keyboard that comes close.

There are a few points to keep in mind as you do your research. If you've followed the explosive growth of the personal computer, you already know that computer technology has advanced amazingly fast over the last three years. Synthesizer technology is no different; every year seems to integrate a new type of audio technology into synthesizers. Generally each new synthesizer technology adds enhancements such as higher-quality sounds and more control. At the same time, these "improvements" can sometimes leave out features that you liked in other keyboards, lose certain sound qualities, and become even more difficult to operate. The move from analog to digital synthesizers is a good example. While some say that digital synthesizers offer more precise control, others argue that analog synthesizers have a fuller and warmer sound than their digital substitutes.

This section will help you start in your search for the synthesizer or controller equipment you need to create or perform your music. In the next few chapters we'll take a look at some of the different types of technology that you'll find on the market, as well as decipher some of the terminology that you'll hear. While we can't cover every type of synthesizer technology, this should give you enough information to understand what is out there: At the very least you'll have a better idea of what you're getting into.

Chapter 14 discusses analog synthesizers, which were the first commercially available synthesizers back in the mid-1960s. You'll find that much of the technology used in today's keyboards comes from these earlier systems. Once you understand some of the concepts behind these original synthesizers, you'll have a better idea of what the various features in today's keyboards can offer you.

Chapter 15 dives right into the ever-changing world of synthesizer technology. Here you'll find descriptions of the most popular synthesizer technologies that came out over the last decade. This information is useful because there are a number of good used keyboards out there that are still based on this technology. Buying the latest and greatest synthesizer is okay for some; however, if you are on a budget you might want to consider some of these earlier technologies and purchase a used keyboard instead of buying one that's brand new.

Finally, Chapter 16 covers MIDI controllers, which enable you to play MIDI synthesizers and sound modules even if you don't play a keyboard. Currently there are MIDI controllers for drummers, guitarists, wind players, and even vocalists; each has its strengths and weaknesses. This last chapter explains how different MIDI controllers work, as well as what to be aware of when considering one for purchase.

Analog Synthesizers: Early Electronic Keyboards

ANALOG SYNTHESIZERS, THE first keyboards that allowed you to precisely adjust the waveform and quality of a sound, have had a profound effect on popular music. In 1968, composer and keyboardist Wendy Carlos used analog synthesizers to set the musical world on its ear with her electronic music album *Switched on Bach*. Carlos performed pieces by J.S. Bach that breathed new life into these classical masterpieces. To say the analog synthesizer caught the public's interest is an understatement; *Switched on Bach* became a nationwide hit and sold more records than any other classical recording of the time. Analog synthesizers quickly found a place in popular music as well, when the lively electronic single "Popcorn" from Hot Butter hit the top 10 charts several years later.

Instead of using precise digital control values, analog synthesizers used electrical voltage as a simple variable control signal. Changing the amount of voltage to a module in an analog synthesizer could change the pitch, brightness of the sound, and trigger various processing modules. To create a sound, you had to patch and cross-patch dozens of cables into the many different modules on a synthesizer, in order to carry the voltage from one module to another. In fact, a synthesizer more closely resembled a telephone switchboard than a piano keyboard in the early days of electronic music. Analog synthesizers in the early 1970s, such as the popular Mini Moog, advanced beyond the modular analog systems by hard wiring many of their functions. These enhancements eliminated the clutter of a thousand and one patch cords. These upgraded synthesizers used sliders, switches, or knobs to route signals, set levels, and process sounds.

Analog synthesizers came in all shapes and sizes; from small, suitcase-sized boxes to monstrous consoles that nearly filled a whole room. In his book *Vintage Synthesizers*, Mark Vail discusses how an enormous analog synthesizer was used in the Steven Spielberg film *Close Encounters of the Third Kind*. According to Vail, during the last part of the movie, a synthesizer keyboard is used to play a melody from a giant spaceship that has landed. A modular analog synthesizer called the ARP 2500 was the specific equipment that produced the melody.

Many of the ways keyboards process and create sounds today are based on the concepts that engineers first developed for analog synthesizers. The *envelope generator*, which controlled many different elements of the sound, is an important example of an original concept for which variations exist today.

An envelope generator can be used to define how fast and the way the sound responds when you play the keyboard by adjusting the ADSR (attack-decay-sustain-release) module. You'll find variations on the early ADSR envelope generator in nearly all of today's synthesizers. The attack setting determines how quickly the note fades in after you touch a key; a percussive sound, such as a marimba, has a fast attack, while a softly bowed cello has a slow attack. The decay defines the time for the signal to go from the peak value to the sustain level (the level at which the sound keeps playing for as long as your finger is on the key). Finally, the release setting determines how long it takes the sound to decay. Short release times are effective when playing percussive instruments, and longer release times are often appropriate for larger ensemble sounds (such as a group of slowly bowed cellos).

How Analog Synthesizers Work

In the early 1960s, Dr. Robert Moog created one of the first and most popular modular synthesizers. Moog synthesizers were modular systems that varied in size according to the whim of the customer; the smaller systems were just the size of a small suitcase, while some were truly gigantic. For example, Keith Emerson of Emerson Lake and Palmer at one time toured with a Moog system that was over 4 feet tall, 4 feet deep, and weighed over 500 pounds. Wendy Carlos used an extensive Moog synthesizer system to produce her album *Switched on Bach*. She also used this system to create the soundtrack for the Stanley Kubrick film *A Clockwork Orange*. In the early seventies, Dr. Moog went on to create one of the most popular analog synthesizers ever, a hard-wired analog synthesizer called the Mini Moog. These analog synthesizers used a method of creating sounds called subtractive synthesis.

How Subtractive Synthesis Works

1 When you press down on the keyboard of an analog synthesizer, you are completing an electrical circuit: the appropriate electrical signal for that key is created by this connection and is sent to the VCO (voltage controlled oscillator).

2 The resulting sound is generated in the VCO as simple waveforms, such as the pure tone of a sine wave or the buzz of a sawtooth wave. To get a fuller sound, it was common to trigger several VCOs at one time.

3 The VCF (voltage controlled filter) eliminated or enhanced certain frequencies produced by the waveforms of the VCOs. VCFs could brighten or dull a sound by boosting or subtracting various frequencies within the sound.

4 The VCA (voltage controlled amplifier) changes gain and is driven by an envelope generator, which sends out a control signal that you can apply to many aspects of a sound. For example, the signal can control how quickly the sound plays, how bright it is, and its overall volume. In electronic music terms, an *envelope* is a shape that changes over time, which you control by defining a set of rate (or time) and level parameters in the envelope generator.

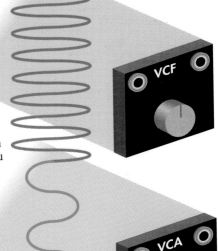

To hear more about analog synthesizers, play track 2 on the audio CD for an interviews with Dr. Robert Moog, Wendy Carlos of *Switched on Bach* fame, and Larry Fast of Synergy. For an example of electronic music at its finest, play track 3; here you'll hear "Legacy," a rare excerpt from the Synergy album *Electronic Realizations for Rock Orchestra*.

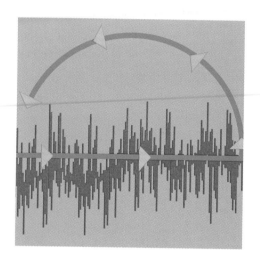

Synthesizer Technology

THERE HAVE BEEN many different types of synthesizer, or synth, technology over the last two decades, but there are five main types of synthesis that you should know about. Analog synthesizers relied on subtractive synthesis to create sounds. In subtractive synthesis you use filters to alter a waveform's harmonic content, thus changing its brightness. This form of synthesis limited the complexity of sounds that you could create, which explains why analog synthesizers have such a distinctive sound. True, some of the giant modular systems could create very complex sounds; however, they required many different modules and equally complex patching.

FM *(Frequency Modulation)* synthesis was developed at Stanford University in California, and it was the technology behind Yamaha's popular DX7 synthesizer. Like subtractive synthesis, FM synthesis was a major breakthrough in synthesizer technology. Today you'll still find FM synthesis at work in Creative Labs's Sound Blaster sound cards for PCs, as well as many Yamaha keyboards and sound modules. FM synthesis is known for two things: sparkling, harmonically complex sounds, and being difficult to program. Many musicians find programming sounds using FM synthesis far from intuitive, and it often takes many hours to get just the right sound.

Roland's *LA (Linear Arithmetic) synthesis* is another popular synthesizer technology that's still available. LA synthesis is limited to the variety of Roland products, including sound modules and keyboards that are still on the market. Popularized by the D-50 keyboard, LA synthesis was legendary for its bright, bell-like textures.

Sample playback is one of the most popular synthesizer technologies around today. Unlike dedicated sampling keyboards, which can *record* digital audio, sample playback modules or keyboards *play back* digital recordings of instruments from the unit's ROM (Read Only Memory) chips. While you can't create new waveforms using sample playback keyboards, you can use filters and other on-board processing to change the quality of the sound. The main benefit to units such as Emu Systems's popular Proteus/1 module is that the sounds are very realistic; after all, they are a recording of the real thing.

Physical modeling is the latest and greatest type of synthesizer technology to hit the market. Physical modeling is different from any other type of synthesis because it literally creates a mathematical model of what an instrument should sound like. Unlike sample playback systems that can only play back a specific digital recording, a physical model of an instrument can change to match the performers' articulations. This makes it possible to create extremely realistic nuances, such as blowing softly into a flute or the pressure of lips on a mouthpiece. Naturally, physical modeling relies quite heavily on computer processing to create its sounds. Yamaha was the first vendor to produce a commercial physical modeling synth, the VL-1. Because of the heavy data processing required for physical modeling, it will be some time before the cost of this technology comes down to an affordable level.

So, of all the technologies I've mentioned here, which one is best? That's something you'll just have to hear for yourself. Some are better than others for certain instruments or sounds. After listening to dozens of different keyboards for over ten years, I can honestly say no one technology is better than the other. Perhaps the most important things you should look for in a keyboard are how it sounds, its ease of operation, and the cost—exactly in that order. If you pick a keyboard that is too expensive, don't worry about it; at least you'll learn your preferences. After you figure these out, just find a keyboard that has many of the same features, but fits into your budget.

Understanding Synthesizer Technology

FM Synthesis:

FM synthesis creates sounds by using one or more operators or oscillators to affect the remaining sound operators. Yamaha's popular DX7 keyboard had six operators, while most sound boards have only two. Each operator (the FM synthesis term for oscillator) has three main parts: a sine wave generator to create the sound, an envelope generator, and an amplitude controller.

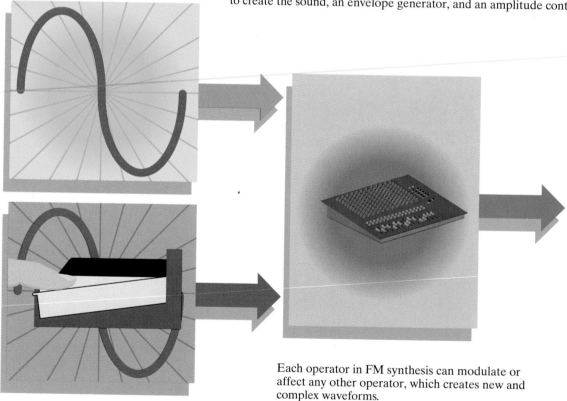

Each operator in FM synthesis can modulate or affect any other operator, which creates new and complex waveforms.

LA Synthesis:

Roland's LA synthesis combines digital audio and synthesizer technologies to create sounds. LA synthesizers use digital recordings of sounds called PCM (pulse coded modulation) samples, as well as synthesized waveforms, and mix these in a variety of patterns. For example, the digital recordings of the beginnings of sounds, such as the pluck of a guitar, could be combined with a synthesized organlike waveform to create a sound that has a sharp attack but a clear, sustained tone.

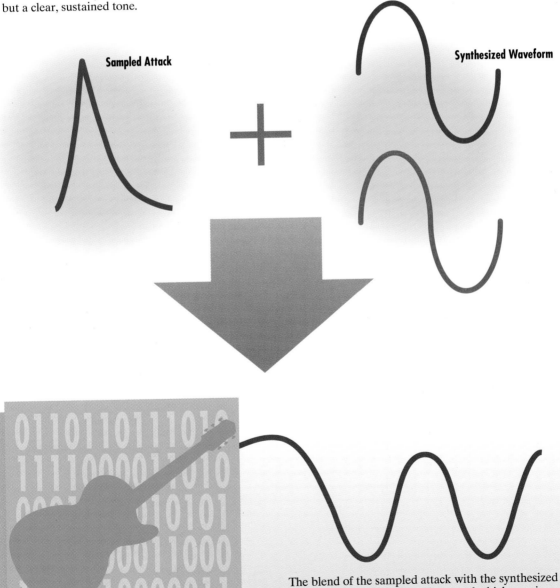

Sampled Attack

Synthesized Waveform

The blend of the sampled attack with the synthesized waveform creates a composite sound which requires very little sample memory.

How Sample Playback Systems Work

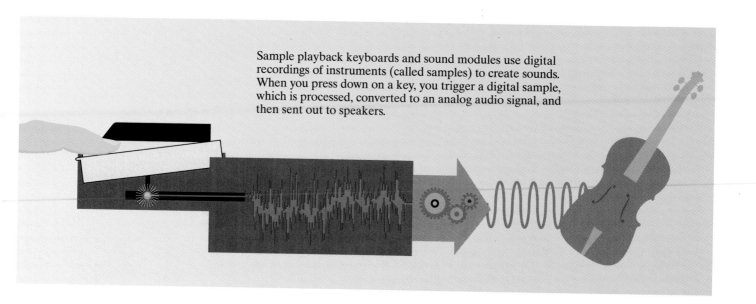

Sample playback keyboards and sound modules use digital recordings of instruments (called samples) to create sounds. When you press down on a key, you trigger a digital sample, which is processed, converted to an analog audio signal, and then sent out to speakers.

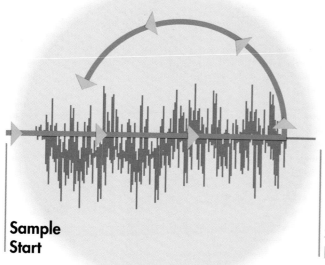

Sample Start

Sample End

Instead of recording several minutes of an instrument, most sample playback systems use a system called looping to create a sustained sound. *Looping* lets you extend the length of a sample by having it repeat a certain portion indefinitely. After you trigger a sound, the loop sends the sound playback signal back to a preset spot somewhere before the end of the sample, and continues playing. This allows you to sustain notes indefinitely without using up too much storage space on your system.

Multisampling is another trick that sample playback systems use. Instead of just playing one sample over the entire range of the keyboard, many sample playback keyboards or modules use multisampled instruments, or instruments with many prerecorded notes. Multisampling keeps the notes from shifting abnormally in pitch and duration.

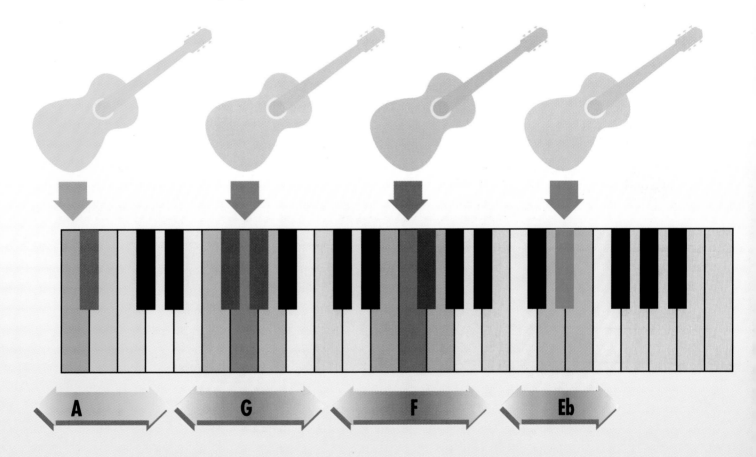

If you are playing a guitar, the original recordings of the guitar are located in primary samples. Primary samples correspond to the main samples at A, G, F, and E flat on the keyboard. Playing a primary sample a few notes above or below its original pitch adds to the realistic production of the instrument's sound, and it doesn't shift the duration of the note abnormally.

To hear multisampling at work, play track 4 on the audio CD.

How Physical Modeling Works

The Yamaha VL-1 was the first physical modeling keyboard available. The $5,000 price tag and its ability to play only two notes at a time has made the VL-1 primarily a tool for the music industry's elite. However, as the cost of special processing chips goes down, you can expect to see a number of less expensive physical modeling keyboards emerge on the market.

To get a better idea of what physical modeling sounds like, listen to track 7 on the audio CD, which gives a demo of Yamaha's VL-1 synthesizer.

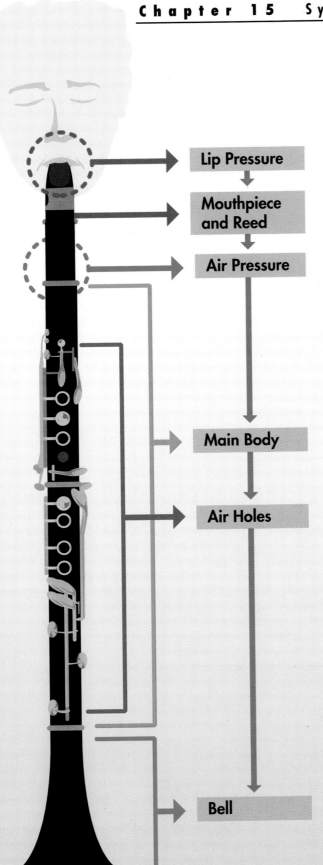

Lip Pressure

Mouthpiece and Reed

Air Pressure

Main Body

Air Holes

Bell

Like a regular instrument, a physical model changes its sound characteristics according to a variety of factors. A physical model of a clarinet, for example, has to map out several variables. You have to take into account how hard the lips and mouth are biting down on the reed, the strength of the mouthpiece and reed, and finally the amount of air pressure you are sending through the mouthpiece. Next you'll need to determine the timbre of the main body, and then how the air holes change not only pitch but the character of the sound. Lastly, the size of the bell at the end of the clarinet also determines how the instrument will sound when played. Once all of these factors have been mapped out, any change in these variables will affect each of the other factors in the same way that they would on a real instrument.

MIDI Controllers

JUST BECAUSE YOU can't play a piano keyboard doesn't mean you are left in the dust when it comes to benefitting from MIDI technology. MIDI controllers can provide a viable alternative for guitarists, drummers, reed instrument players, and others who want to use their current instrument to play MIDI sound modules. MIDI controllers don't actually play any sound; instead, they convert your performance to MIDI data that any MIDI instrument can receive.

There are MIDI controllers for guitars, drums, wind instruments, and many other instruments. Each controller is unique to the type of instrument that it is emulating. Early guitar synthesizers used custom guitars as the main controller, but current guitar synthesizers, especially those from Roland, are primarily devices that you add onto your existing guitar. For example, Roland's GR-1 synthesizer/GK1 interface combination adds a small box to the bridge of your guitar, and allows you to switch between straight guitar, synthesized sounds, or a combination of both. This signal then feeds a converter that drives an internal sound generator, and can also send MIDI data to other synthesizers.

Vocalists, brass players, and others can use Pitch-To-MIDI converters, which convert their acoustic energy to MIDI data. There's even a MIDI controller for tap shoes! Actor and dancer Gregory Hines wore a pair of custom tap shoes in making the film *Tap* in 1989. The shoes had MIDI triggers on them. As Hines danced, the triggers would send signals to various MIDI keyboards and sound modules, which were mixed with the sound of the tap shoes.

Yet having a MIDI controller and synthesizer or tone module that can create MIDI sounds is only half the battle; how you *play* the sounds is as important as their quality. Because of the difficulty in precisely emulating the way instruments feel, each type of MIDI controller has individual quirks that you'll need to adjust to. Guitarists may find that they need to slow down passages and pluck strings more precisely in order to get a clean tone; drummers may have to compensate for the small amount of delay that occurs between hitting the pad and when the MIDI instrument actually plays the sound; the feel and the weight of the plastic body on many wind controllers can throw traditional woodwind instrumentalists for a loop.

However, when you finally get comfortable with the controller and properly adjust all the settings in your MIDI equipment, the musical effect can be stunning. A performance that Laurie Anderson gave is one example of this that comes to mind. She used MIDI technology to play a violin onstage. When she drew the bow across the violin during the opening of one concert, instead of just one violin, the audience was surprised by a barrage of instruments playing at the same time.

On a smaller scale, MIDI controllers can make a nice, subtle addition to your current playing setup, especially since guitarists and drummers can use their original instruments as the main controller. A little MIDI enhancement can go a long way. You may only use the MIDI controller infrequently; but when you need it, nothing else will do.

Drum and Guitar MIDI Controllers

1 Drum controllers convert each strike of the drum stick into MIDI note on-and-off information, as well as velocity information. Each drum controller handles the process a little differently, but the basic idea is the same.

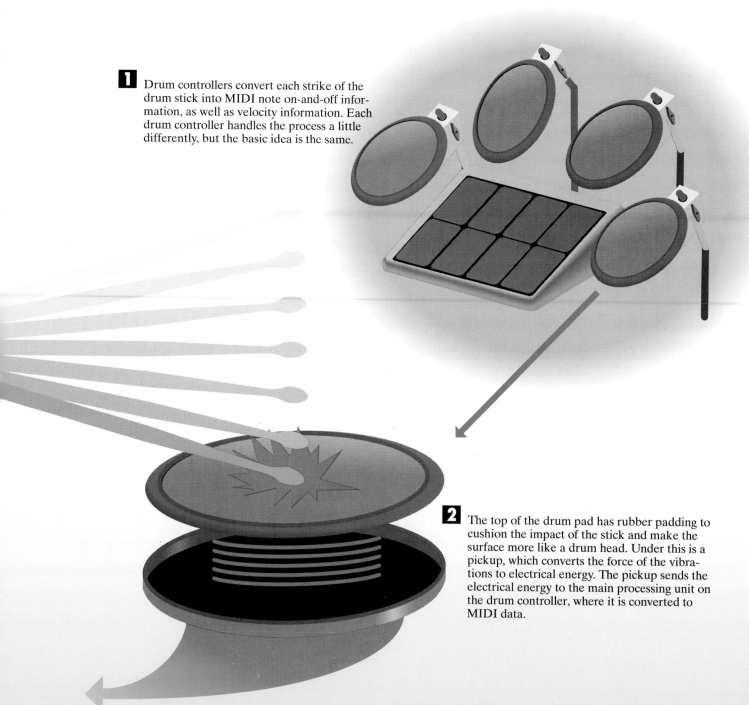

2 The top of the drum pad has rubber padding to cushion the impact of the stick and make the surface more like a drum head. Under this is a pickup, which converts the force of the vibrations to electrical energy. The pickup sends the electrical energy to the main processing unit on the drum controller, where it is converted to MIDI data.

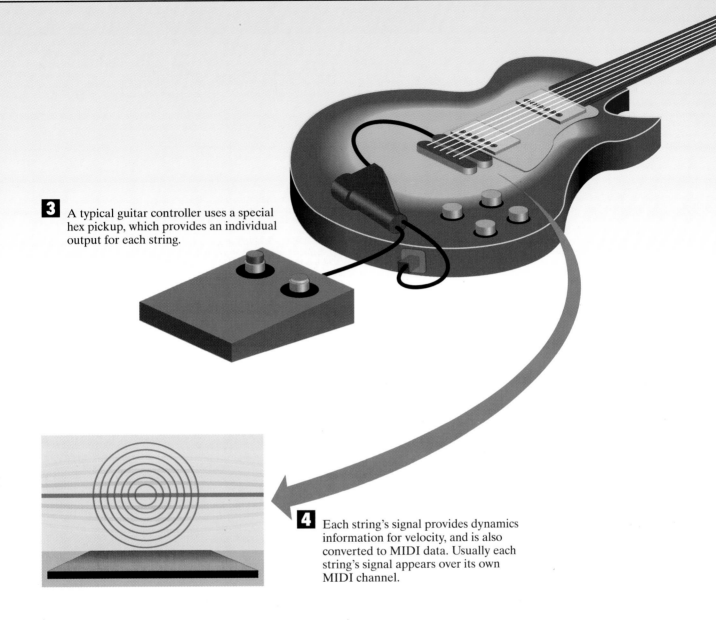

3 A typical guitar controller uses a special hex pickup, which provides an individual output for each string.

4 Each string's signal provides dynamics information for velocity, and is also converted to MIDI data. Usually each string's signal appears over its own MIDI channel.

To hear what a guitar controller sounds like, play track 12 on the audio CD, which has a demonstration of a guitar controller by author and composer Craig Anderton.

How a Wind Controller Works

Wind controllers, such as Yamaha's WX11, are very similar to regular wind instruments; you blow into them, change pitch by tightening your lips on the reed, and even use standard saxophone and flute fingering. The main difference is that wind controllers don't make any sound on their own. You have to hook up a wind controller to a MIDI sound module in order to produce any sound.

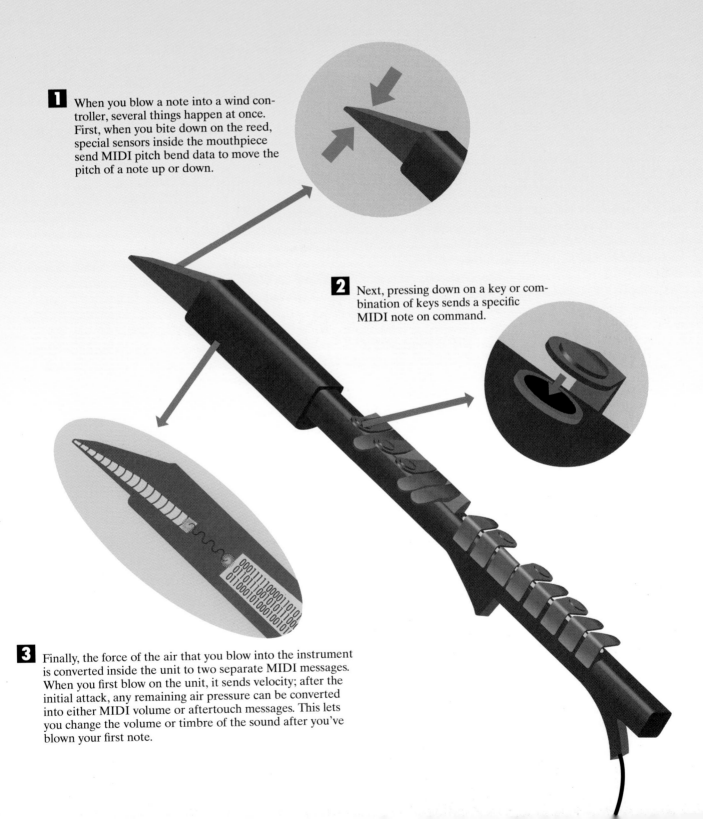

1 When you blow a note into a wind controller, several things happen at once. First, when you bite down on the reed, special sensors inside the mouthpiece send MIDI pitch bend data to move the pitch of a note up or down.

2 Next, pressing down on a key or combination of keys sends a specific MIDI note on command.

3 Finally, the force of the air that you blow into the instrument is converted inside the unit to two separate MIDI messages. When you first blow on the unit, it sends velocity; after the initial attack, any remaining air pressure can be converted into either MIDI volume or aftertouch messages. This lets you change the volume or timbre of the sound after you've blown your first note.

How a Theremin Works

The theremin is a unique instrument that few people have seen, yet it remains one of the most interesting ways to create music. Developed by Leon Theremin in 1928, the theremin produces a haunting sound very reminiscent of the human voice, yet very distinctive at the same time. You can hear its haunting sound in the Beach Boy's hit single "Good Vibrations." Updated versions of these classic instruments can also serve as MIDI controllers.

To change the pitch on the theremin, you move your hand toward or away from the pitch antenna, which stands straight up from the top of the unit. When your hand is about 2 feet away, the instrument plays a tone that is in the same range as the lowest note on a cello. Bringing your hand within a half inch of the pitch antenna raises it to its highest note. MIDI theremins, such as the Big Briar Series 91 theremin, also send note on and pitch bend information when your hand moves toward the pitch antenna.

To control the volume, you move your hand toward or away from the volume antenna. When your hand is close to the volume antenna, the instrument doesn't play any sound; as you move your hand back, the volume increases. Theremins that use MIDI send out MIDI volume control information while modulating the sound.

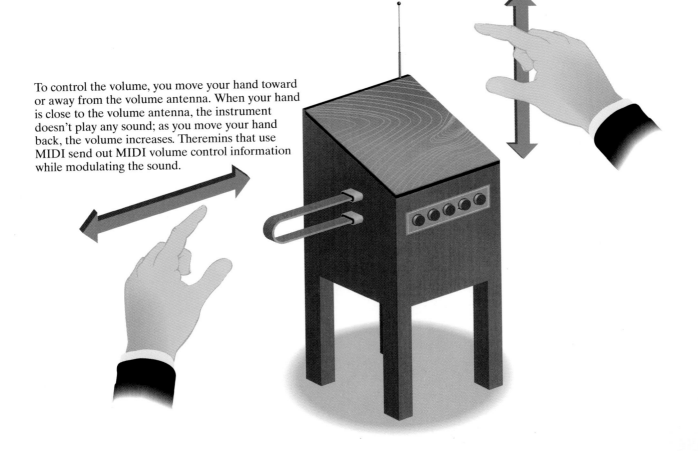

Because the sound of a theremin is so unique, track 8 contains a demonstration of how to play one. This track also includes an excerpt from a performance by a top-notch theremin performer.

Appendix: About the CD

Although the marriage of computers and music has had a profound effect on the music and entertainment industry, this union won't seem very impressive if you can't *hear* the results. That's why I've created this audio CD with many examples of computer music technology at work. You'll hear interviews with some of the top people in the electronic music industry; demonstrations of electronic instruments and technologies; and musical examples that help tie everything together.

By the way, you don't need a computer to play this CD; this CD is exactly the same as a compact disc that you buy in a music store. However, you can play this CD back in a CD-ROM drive if you have the appropriate audio CD driver for your system.

This CD was designed as a companion piece for the book, so many of the basic concepts and technologies you'll hear discussed are also covered in the text. When icons appear at the bottom of illustrated pages, this indicates that there are counterparts on the CD. These icons will direct you to the number of the related track on the CD, and tell you a bit about what you'll hear when you play that track. Feel free to listen to all of the CD, or just the tracks you're interested in. Enjoy!

What's on the CD

Track 1: Introduction—How to Use This CD

Track 2: Early Electronic Music Summit

This is an interview with some of the main people that made electronic-music history: Dr. Moog, inventor of the world's first commercial synthesizer; Wendy Carlos of *Switched-on Bach* fame; and Larry Fast of Synergy. Moog, Carlos, and Fast talk about some of the origins, early resistance, and benefits of electronic music.

Track 3: "Legacy"

This is a rare example of electronic music at its finest from Larry Fast's first Synergy album, *Electronic Realizations for Rock Orchestra*.

Track 4: Sampling Mania

A demonstration of digital audio sampling technology.

Track 5: Creating a Hit Single

Four-time Grammy nominee Thomas Dolby talks about how he used digital audio, MIDI, and computer technology to create his hit single, "I Love You, Good-bye" from his album *Astronauts and Heretics.*

Track 6: Creating Movie Sound Effects

A demonstration and interview with top sound designer Alan Howarth on how he creates film sound effects.

Track 7: Physical Modeling

A demonstration of the Yamaha VL-1, one of the first commercial physical modeling synthesizers available.

Track 8: Meet the Theremin

A demonstration on how you play a theremin, featuring Dr. Robert Moog.

Track 9: 3D Audio

A demonstration of what 3D audio sounds like, featuring Dr. Durand R. Begault.

Track 10: MIDI Sequencing

A demonstration of how MIDI Sequencing works.

Track 11: "Waltz for Llysa"

An original composition that I wrote for my friend Llysa Holland for her wedding, this piece uses MIDI and digital audio technologies.

Track 12: Guitar Controllers

A demonstration on the pros and cons of working with a guitar controller, featuring author, composer, and guitarist Craig Anderton.

About the Artists

Craig Anderton   A legend in the music industry, Craig Anderton has written extensively about electronic music technology for over 25 years. As a musician, Craig has performed at Carnegie Hall. He has also recorded albums with new-age artists Spencer Brewer and David Arkenstone.

Dr. Durand R. Begault   The author of *3D sound for Virtual Reality and Multimedia,* Dr. Durand R. Begault is one of the top acoustic research scientists at NASA Ames Research

Center. In his free time, Dr. Begault mysteriously transforms into Randy Begault, the dynamite jazz pianist for the infamous Lars Mars Orchestra.

Wendy Carlos   Keyboardist and composer Wendy Carlos is probably best known for turning the electronic music world on its ear with *Switched-on Bach*, one of the most popular electronic music records ever made. In addition to many classical electronic music recordings, Wendy has also written and performed the film scores for *A Clockwork Orange, The Shining,* and *Tron.*

Thomas Dolby   Four-time Grammy nominee Thomas Dolby has put out four hit albums and top ten singles, including "Blinded by Science," "Europa and the Pirate Twins," "Hyperactive," and "I Love You, Good-bye." As a session keyboardist and producer, Thomas has worked with many different artists, including Joni Mitchell, Foreigner, and the Thompson Twins.

Larry Fast   Larry Fast is perhaps best known for his nine ground-breaking electronic music albums under the name Synergy. The Synergy albums are an exquisite blend of electronic music technology and traditional musical composition technique. Larry has also worked extensively with Peter Gabriel for more than a decade, playing synthesizer on his albums and on tour. In addition, Larry has many credits as a session synthesist, working for Kate Bush, Hall & Oates, Randy Newman, Meatloaf, and Shadowfax, among others.

Erik Holsinger   Erik Holsinger is an independent audio, video, and CD-ROM producer based in San Francisco, California. As a writer, Erik has covered the computer-based video, audio, and multimedia markets for over eight years in dozens of articles for *MacWEEK, PC World, Digital Video, Millimeter, New Media,* and *Wired* magazines. As a composer, Erik's musical scores have aired on national commercials, PBS, and award-winning independent films.

Alan Howarth   Composer and sound designer Alan Howarth has worked with director John Carpenter on the scores for *Big Trouble in Little China, Escape from New York,* and *Halloween 2* through *5.* As a sound effects designer, Alan has created sound effects for dozens of major motion pictures, including all the *Star Trek* films, *The Hunt for Red October, The Little Mermaid, Poltergeist,* Francis Ford Coppola's *Dracula,* and *The Mask.*

Dr. Bob Moog   Dr. Moog got the electronic music scene started when he designed and created the first commercial synthesizer in the late 1960s. Formerly the head of Moog Music, Bob is now the president of Big Briar, Inc., an Ashville, North Carolina company that specializes in building innovative music instruments, such as MIDI-controlled theremins.

Credits

How Music and Computers Work Audio CD

Written and produced by Erik Holsinger

Recorded at Electric Melody Studios in Burbank, California; Whitewater Recording in Ashville, North Carolina; Synergy Electronic Music Studios in Newark, New Jersey; and Earwax Productions in San Francisco, California.

Engineered at Earwax Productions in San Francisco.

Dialog direction and main engineering by Barney Jones of Earwax Productions.

Additional engineering: Peter Steinbach, Earwax Productions; Adam Greenberg, Whitewater Recording

All music composed and performed by Erik Holsinger and ©1994 by Erik Holsinger/Musical Imagery, except for:

"Legacy" (Track 3), written and performed by Larry Fast of Synergy® Electronic Music Inc.

Guitar Controller Demo (Track 12), written and performed by Craig Anderton.

Software used during the production of the audio CD:
Digital Audio and MIDI sequencing: Opcode's Studio Vision Pro; MIDI sequencing: Mark of the Unicorn's Performer; music notation: Passport Design's Encore; digital audio editing: Sound Designer II from Digidesign; digital audio processing (compression, equalization, limiting): Sound Designer II and L1-Ultraharmonizer from k.s. Waves Ltd.; digital audio mixing: DECK II from OSC and Digidesign's Pro Tools; CD audio disk mastering: Digidesign's MasterList. SampleCell II CD-ROM collections used: Digidesign's SampleCell II (volumes one and two), Miroslav Vitous Virtual Symphony, OSC's Poke in the Ear with a Sharp Stick (volumes two and three) and Textural Ambience, Invision Interactive's Lightware Sample Cell Collection (volume one); data backup: DATa from Digidesign and Retrospect from Danz Development

Thomas Dolby appears courtesy of Giant Records. "I Love You, Good-bye," Lost Toy People Inc., administered by Warner Music Corp. (ASCAP)

Larry Fast appears courtesy of Synergy® Electronic Music, Inc.

All Rights Reserved. Unauthorized duplication is a violation of applicable laws.

ATTENTION TEACHERS AND TRAINERS
Now You Can Teach From These Books!

ZD Press now offers instructors and trainers
the materials they need to use these books in their classes.

- An Instructor's Manual features flexible lessons designed for use in a 10- or 15-week course (30-45 course hours).

- Student exercises and tests on floppy disk provide you with an easy way to tailor and/or duplicate tests as you need them.

- A Transparency Package contains all the graphics from the book, each on a single, full-color transparency.

- Spanish edition of *PC/Computing How Computers Work* is available.

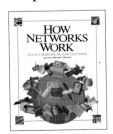

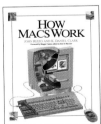

These materials are available only to qualified accounts. For more information contact:

Corporations, Government Agencies: Cindy Johnson, 800-488-8741, ext. 108

In the U.S.A: Academic Institutions: Suzanne Anthony, 800-786-6541, ext. 108

In Canada: Copp Clark Pitman Ltd.

In the U.K.: The Computer Bookshops

In Australia: WoodLane Pty. Ltd.

ZIFF-DAVIS
ZD
PRESS

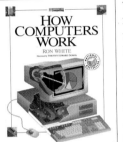
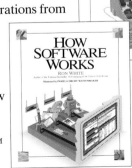

Ziff-Davis Press Survey of Readers

Please help us in our effort to produce the best books on personal computing.
For your assistance, we would be pleased to send you a FREE catalog
featuring the complete line of Ziff-Davis Press books.

1. How did you first learn about this book?

Recommended by a friend . . . . ☐ -1 (5)

Recommended by store personnel . . . . ☐ -2

Saw in Ziff-Davis Press catalog . . . . ☐ -3

Received advertisement in the mail . . . . ☐ -4

Saw the book on bookshelf at store . . . . ☐ -5

Read book review in: _____ ☐ -6

Saw an advertisement in: _____ ☐ -7

Other (Please specify): _____ ☐ -8

2. Which THREE of the following factors most influenced your decision to purchase this book? (Please check up to THREE.)

Front or back cover information on book . . .☐ -1 (6)

Logo of magazine affiliated with book . . . . . .☐ -2

Special approach to the content . . . .☐ -3

Completeness of content . . . .☐ -4

Author's reputation. . . . .☐ -5

Publisher's reputation . . . .☐ -6

Book cover design or layout . . . .☐ -7

Index or table of contents of book . . . .☐ -8

Price of book . . . .☐ -9

Special effects, graphics, illustrations . . . . . .☐ -0

Other (Please specify): _____ ☐ -x

3. How many computer books have you purchased in the last six months? _____ (7-10)

4. On a scale of 1 to 5, where 5 is excellent, 4 is above average, 3 is average, 2 is below average, and 1 is poor, please rate each of the following aspects of this book below. (Please circle your answer.)

Depth/completeness of coverage	5	4	3	2	1	(11)
Organization of material	5	4	3	2	1	(12)
Ease of finding topic	5	4	3	2	1	(13)
Special features/time saving tips	5	4	3	2	1	(14)
Appropriate level of writing	5	4	3	2	1	(15)
Usefulness of table of contents	5	4	3	2	1	(16)
Usefulness of index	5	4	3	2	1	(17)
Usefulness of accompanying disk	5	4	3	2	1	(18)
Usefulness of illustrations/graphics	5	4	3	2	1	(19)
Cover design and attractiveness	5	4	3	2	1	(20)
Overall design and layout of book	5	4	3	2	1	(21)
Overall satisfaction with book	5	4	3	2	1	(22)

5. Which of the following computer publications do you read regularly; that is, 3 out of 4 issues?

Byte . . . . ☐ -1 (23)

Computer Shopper . . . . ☐ -2

Corporate Computing . . . . ☐ -3

Dr. Dobb's Journal . . . . ☐ -4

LAN Magazine . . . . ☐ -5

MacWEEK . . . . ☐ -6

MacUser . . . . ☐ -7

PC Computing . . . .☐ -8

PC Magazine . . . . ☐ -9

PC WEEK . . . . ☐ -0

Windows Sources . . . . ☐ -x

Other (Please specify): _____ ☐ -y

Please turn page.

6. What is your level of experience with personal computers? With the subject of this book?

	With PCs	With subject of book
Beginner.	☐ -1 (24)	☐ -1 (25)
Intermediate.	☐ -2	☐ -2
Advanced.	☐ -3	☐ -3

7. Which of the following best describes your job title?

Officer (CEO/President/VP/owner). . . . . . . ☐ -1 (26)
Director/head. . . . . ☐ -2
Manager/supervisor. ☐ -3
Administration/staff. . . . . ☐ -4
Teacher/educator/trainer. . . . . ☐ -5
Lawyer/doctor/medical professional. . . . . . . ☐ -6
Engineer/technician. ☐ -7
Consultant. . . . . ☐ -8
Not employed/student/retired. . . . . ☐ -9
Other (Please specify): _____ ☐ -0

8. What is your age?

Under 20. . . . . ☐ -1 (27)
21-29. . . . . ☐ -2
30-39. . . . . ☐ -3
40-49. . . . . ☐ -4
50-59. . . . . ☐ -5
60 or over. . . . . ☐ -6

9. Are you:

Male. . . . . ☐ -1 (28)
Female. . . . . ☐ -2

Thank you for your assistance with this important information! Please write your address below to receive our free catalog.

Name: _____

Address: _____

City/State/Zip: _____

Fold here to mail.

215X-13-08

Credits

How Music and Computers Work Audio CD

Written and produced by Erik Holsinger

Recorded at Electric Melody Studios in Burbank, California; Whitewater Recording in Ashville, North Carolina; Synergy Electronic Music Studios in Newark, New Jersey; and Earwax Productions in San Francisco, California.

Engineered at Earwax Productions in San Francisco.

Dialog direction and main engineering by Barney Jones of Earwax Productions.

Additional engineering: Peter Steinbach, Earwax Productions; Adam Greenberg, Whitewater Recording

All music composed and performed by Erik Holsinger and ©1994 by Erik Holsinger/Musical Imagery, except for:

"Legacy" (Track 3), written and performed by Larry Fast of Synergy® Electronic Music Inc.

Guitar Controller Demo (Track 12), written and performed by Craig Anderton.

Software used during the production of the audio CD:
Digital Audio and MIDI sequencing: Opcode's Studio Vision Pro; MIDI sequencing: Mark of the Unicorn's Performer; music notation: Passport Design's Encore; digital audio editing: Sound Designer II from Digidesign; digital audio processing (compression, equalization, limiting): Sound Designer II and L1-Ultraharmonizer from k.s. Waves Ltd.; digital audio mixing: DECK II from OSC and Digidesign's Pro Tools; CD audio disk mastering: Digidesign's MasterList. SampleCell II CD-ROM collections used: Digidesign's SampleCell II (volumes one and two), Miroslav Vitous Virtual Symphony, OSC's Poke in the Ear with a Sharp Stick (volumes two and three) and Textural Ambience, Invision Interactive's Lightware Sample Cell Collection (volume one); data backup: DATa from Digidesign and Retrospect from Danz Development

Thomas Dolby appears courtesy of Giant Records. "I Love You, Good-bye," Lost Toy People Inc., administered by Warner Music Corp. (ASCAP)

Larry Fast appears courtesy of Synergy® Electronic Music, Inc.